LIFE OF A SCIENTIST

D.S. Tselnik

My Life in the USSR and the USA

Injustice and Other Recollections

Third Edition
Further Expanded

Published by David Tselnik

Fargo, North Dakota, USA

Printed in the United States of America

Library of Congress Control Number: 2018914240

Copyright © 2019 by David Tselnik.
All rights reserved. No part of this publication may be reproduced, stored in a retrieval system, or transmitted, in any form or by any means, electronic, mechanical, photocopying, recording, or otherwise, without the prior written permission of the copyright holder.

ISBN 978-0-9837324-2-6

D. S. Tselnik

22 June 2019.

Preface to the Third Edition

I am Dr. David Tselnik, and this is the Third Edition of the book "Life of a Scientist: My Life in the USSR and the USA," a book about my life.

There are two parts in this edition of the book.

Part One, "Injustice," is mostly about my education and my professional life. This part consists of two chapters. Chapter One contains a description of a number of events in my life in the USSR, and Chapter Two - a description of a number of events in my life in the USA.

Part Two, "Other Recollections," is a kaleidoscope of descriptions of various events in my life, in the lives of my grandparents and parents, in the lives of some other people (whom I knew, or whom the people whom I knew well knew), and this part also contains some material of a general nature helpful in understanding other material in the book. Part Two consists of four chapters, Chapter Three - Chapter Six.

There is also a separate Section "In Conclusion," three Appendices, Glossary (pages 237-239), and References (page 240) in this edition of the book.

As a result of adding new material, the length of the book

increased from 172 pages in the second edition to 252 pages in this, the third one.

   The book is written for the general reader. I entertain a hope that you will read this book in its entirety, from cover to cover, and that you will find the contents of this book interesting.

   I would also like to express my gratitude to Ms. Robin Mangino, who shared with me her thoughts about the second edition of this book, and who sent me a list of places where (in the second edition) corrections - mostly small - were necessary.

With Best Wishes,

D.S. Tselnik.

December 2018.

From the Preface to the Second Edition

As a result of adding new material, the length of the book increased from 97 pages in the first edition to 172 pages in the second edition.

The readers of the first edition were telling me that the book was easy to read, and also that reading that book was like talking with me.

Ms. Robin Mangino (of West Caldwell, NJ) sent me a list of about a dozen places in the first edition of the book where small corrections, of mostly typos, were needed. For that, I want to thank Ms. Mangino.

December 2017.

From the Preface to the First Edition

I am seventy six years of age now. Of these seventy six years, for the first forty years I lived in the USSR, and for the thirty six years after that, I lived - and I am living now - in the USA.

This book consists of two chapters: Chapter One contains description of a number of events in my life in the USSR, and Chapter Two - description of a number of events in my life in the USA.

In addition to the two chapters, the book also contains Glossary ... , and References ... .

Most of the material in Chapter One in this book, and in

the Glossary, too, is borrowed from my book "Six Chapters on Series Expansions," which I self-published in 2012 (see Ref. [5, pages 363-381]); the material of Chapter Two is new - completely.

I am not a writer by profession, and the reason that I wrote this book is simply that I felt the need to share some of my experiences in life with other people.

October 2013.

Part One

INJUSTICE

Chapter 1

In The USSR

My Parents and Grandparents

My father was a teacher of mathematics by profession, educated at the Odessa State University, in Odessa, a city on the shore of the Black Sea, in the Ukraine. My mother, by profession, was an economist. She spent her student years in Moscow, then in Kiev (where she studied the English language), and, finally, in Odessa, where she studied credit and finance at the Odessa Institute of Credit and Economy.

Mother and Father met each other at a high school in Odessa. Mother was approaching the school building - she came to submit her application for enrollment - and she saw a boy, with dark hair and brown eyes, who was explaining something to a few fellow applicants. It turned out that he was explaining something mathematical to them. That was my future father.

Neither my father nor my mother were born in Odessa. My father was born in 1910 in the town of Rybnitsa, situated on the left bank of the Dniester river, in Moldavia. Moldavia - and the Ukraine too - were at that time parts of the Russian Empire, later - Republics in the Soviet Union, and now they both are independent countries: the Republic of Moldova and Ukraine.

My father's parents, my grandfather Shlema and my grandmother Enia, owned and operated a general store in the town of Rybnitsa, and my father, in his free (from school and homework) time, helped them in the store. Since a very young age, my father wanted to become a teacher of mathematics. When he was fifteen, his parents sent him to Odessa, to continue his education in a big city.

My mother was born in 1909 in Belostok, Poland - which was then a part of the Russian Empire too. My mother's father, Ovsei, was a bukhgalter (accountant, book-keeper), and her mother, Hana, was a housewife. By the standards of her time, my grandmother Hana was an educated woman. As far as I know, she was a gymnasium (secondary school, high school) graduate. Mother's family moved to Odessa in 1914, after the beginning of the First World War.

My mother and father were pupils in the same class in their high school. Mathematics played a decisive role in how they started dating. My mother became ill (the flu maybe), and she missed a considerable number of classes. She then came to their teacher of mathematics and told him that she needed help. He suggested that she should ask the boy who was the best in mathematics in her class to help her. She asked. He helped her. Then - they started dating. That boy was my future father. He was fifteen then, and she was sixteen ...

Remark. *The meaning of the word* Class (in School) *in the USSR was not completely identical to the meaning of the same word in the USA. The difference is explained in the section* Meanings of the Word Class (in School) *in Chapter 6 of the book.*

1937 - I Am Born; 1939 - Our Family Moves to Moscow

At the time I was born, in 1937, my parents lived and worked in Kamenets-Podolsk, a city in the (Western)

Ukraine.

One day my mother, who had previously lived for a period of time (when she was a student) in Moscow, and later spent some time collecting materials for her Diploma Project (and maybe working as an intern too) at the Headquarters of the State Bank of the USSR in Moscow, told my father that she wanted our family to move to Moscow.

None of my parents' friends believed that that was possible. Moscow was the capital of the USSR, and in order to settle in Moscow, a newcomer needed a permit from the militsia (police; there is a Glossary in pages 237-239 of the book) to live in Moscow. But the militsia would not give a newcomer a permit to live in Moscow unless that person had an offer of a job in Moscow. At the same time, no job in Moscow would be offered to a newcomer unless he had a permit from the militsia to live in Moscow. That was a classic case of a vicious circle ("catch 22").

My parents came to Moscow, and Father went to the City Department of Education. There he learned that one of the Moscow schools needed a teacher of mathematics on the high-school level, who at the same time would be willing to serve as the deputy director (deputy principal) of that school. And there was an apartment in the building of that school, on the first floor, with a separate entrance, which was vacant, where the deputy director and his family could live.

The beginning of the academic year (the first of September) was quickly approaching. My father had an excellent education in mathematics for the position (on the Master's degree level), experience, and excellent recommendations.

A telephone call from the Head of the Department of Education of Moscow to the Chief of Militsia of Moscow removed all the obstacles. My father got an excellent job, we had a place to live in Moscow, and the Moscow School System acquired an excellent teacher of mathematics.

After that, my mother went to the Headquarters of the State Bank of the USSR. They knew her, they liked her work, and she was offered a job quickly. We became Muscovites. That all happened in 1939, when I was two-and-a-half years old.

Before the Second World War Started for the USSR

My father and my mother worked, and I was with a nanny, who lived with us. Her name was Anna, but we called her Niura or, tenderly, Niurochka. She was then a young woman, with modest education (she probably finished five or six grades out of ten grades which then constituted the USSR's public school educational system), with a long-long blond hair, and a heart of gold. Niura loved me, and she became friends with my mother and father. (When she was no longer my nanny, her friendship with our family continued.)

The permanent nanny for me, Niura, was not found immediately though. On those occasions when my parents had nobody to sit with me, my father would take me to his class, where I would sit quietly on the lap of one of the pupils, listening, wide-eyed and with open mouth, to my father's teaching of mathematics.

The year 1941 found Father in the position of the director (principal) of his school and teaching mathematics. He planned to go, in the summer, to the Mekhanico-Mathematical Fakul'tet (College of Mechanics and

Mathematics) of the Moscow State University, to take all the necessary papers to apply for enrollment in Aspirantura (the program of studies and research leading to the Kandidat Nauk degree, the USSR's equivalent to the Ph.D. degree in the Western World).

Remark. Fakul'tet *is the word of the Russian language written with the use of the English alphabet (transliterated). The Russian and the English alphabets are, naturally, different. Even the numbers of letters in these two alphabets are not the same: thirty three in the Russian and twenty six in the English alphabet.*

Not every letter of the Russian alphabet has an equivalent in the English alphabet. There is a letter in the Russian alphabet named the "soft sign." That letter, when written after a consonant, directs to pronounce that consonant in a soft manner, softly.

When the Russian words are written with the use of the English alphabet, the soft sign is usually replaced by the apostrophe. And that is what the reader can see in the word Fakul'tet *(and in some other Russian words, and names, written with the use of the English alphabet in this book).*

Germany Invades the Soviet Union. My Father Is Drafted into the Soviet Army; Mother and I Are Evacuated from Moscow

The invasion of the German Army, on the 22nd of June, 1941, into the USSR changed everything. My father was, soon after that, drafted into the Soviet Army, where he spent the next four-and-a-half years. At approximately the same time that my father was drafted into the army, my mother and I were evacuated from Moscow (all the mothers with small children were evacuated). First, we were evacuated to Gor'kii (Gorky; today - Nizhnii Novgorod), a city on the river of Volga, and later we were evacuated further to the East.

Since my father had no prior military training, his rank, when drafted, was private. For a period of time, he served as a field telephonist. Serving in that capacity, Father sometimes had to be situated in the "no man's land," between the Soviet and the German troops. For him, a Jew (both my parents were Jews, and all my grandparents were orthodox Jews), that was especially dangerous: if captured, he would not be taken prisoner, he would be killed on the spot.

Later (I think, that happened sometime in 1942), my father was offered a chance to study artillery, for three months, at the Mikhailovskoe Artillery School. That was a highly respected military school, founded in 1820. Normally, in peacetime, the school functioned in Leningrad (which previously was called Saint Petersburg, and now it is called St. Petersburg again). During the Second World War, the school operated somewhere in the area of the Ural Mountains, and that is where my father spent three months studying artillery.

My mother and I also lived in the area of the Ural Mountains at that time, and my mother and father knew that they were close to each other (by the scale of distances in the Soviet Union, of course; that was a huge country). But they could communicate only by letters.

Three months was the duration of the accelerated course in the School. One should keep in mind, however, that the people who were enrolled in that course were the people with higher education: engineers, mathematicians, etc., not the people just after the high school. They also were experienced soldiers by that time, so all they needed was to study subjects in artillery.

Upon graduation from the School, my father, now a junior lieutenant, became a commander of an artillery unit, in which capacity he served for the rest of his stay in the army. For a period of time, Father was in charge of a unit which had four guns of a smaller caliber. I remember Father mentioned shooting at German tanks: the tanks were advancing, and my father's unit was shooting at them by direct aiming (point-blank).

For another period of time (later, I believe), my father was in charge of a unit which had one gun of a very large caliber. This gun was capable of shooting at very long distances. Aiming was made by computations as the target could not be seen.

....

I do have some memories of the life in the evacuation. Here is one of them.

My grandmother Hana and I were walking along a street in the city of Gor'kii. Suddenly, airplanes appeared in the sky. These were German bombers, coming to bomb the automobile plant. (That plant was built in the city of Gor'kii with the participation of the Ford Motor Company.) I remember that German bombs, when falling, produced terrible noise. That is all I remember of that bombardment. Later, when we lived further to the East, there were no bombardments.

Food was always a problem in the evacuation. Some of the food which we could get was American food: egg powder, milk powder, canned meat. That American food was of great help during the time of war.

Mother and I Return to Moscow; I Enter the First Grade of School

In October of 1943, my mother and I returned to Moscow. Mother wanted me to enter school; she had to work, and she had nobody who could stay with me. Also, every pupil in school was given a bagel every day, and that amounted to six bagels per week - because school was held Monday through Saturday. Maybe some other food was given to pupils in school, that I simply do not remember.

Food was rationed at that time. There was not enough food in the country. A person was allowed to buy only a limited amount of food. These bagels were given to children in school in addition to the ration and for free.

There were two obstacles, however, for me to become a pupil in school. First of all, the school year had already started, on the 1st of September, and we returned to Moscow in the second half of October. Second, and most important, the normal age to enter school was then eight years in the USSR, and I was not even seven.

The school where we had lived (where my father was the director before the war) had become a girls' school, and the boys' school, where I was supposed to become a pupil (the next school year, though), was just nearby. My mother went to the director of that boys' school. He knew my father and our family from the pre-war time, and he agreed to make an exception for me. So I became pupil in the first grade of school - in 1943.

For the first month-and-a-half or two months maybe, my mother checked my homework. That is, every evening she asked me to show her my homework, and if she found, for example, that I did not write something accurately enough, I had to rewrite all the homework anew. The writing was then done by a pen in liquid ink, and it was easy to blot. So I had to be careful.

In addition to that, Mother would ask me questions about the material I had to study, and if I was unable to answer even a single question, I had then to spend additional time studying. Several weeks of such supervision brought the desired results. For the rest of my school years, neither my mother nor my father (after he returned home from army) had to ever look at my homework. They knew that I would control everything myself.

At a Young Age, I Learned That I Could Be Disliked Just for Being a Jew

When I was in the first grade of school (or in the second grade maybe), a certain experience taught me that I could be disliked just for being a Jew.

That is how that happened. Our school building needed repair. So for one semester, our classes were held at a different school, located fifteen, or twenty maybe, minutes of walking from the place where my mother and I lived.

One day, when after school I started walking home, a group of boys, pupils from the same school, surrounded me, and they started beating me. Two adult women were approaching, and when the boys saw them, they all ran away.

The women asked me, "Why were they beating you?" I did not know why, I did not even know those boys, they were from a different class. "What is your name?" asked the women. "David," I answered. "Oh," said the women, "they were beating you because you are a Jew!"

I have to explain that, unlike in the United States, where a considerable number of boys and men of different ethnicities have the first name David, in the USSR only Jewish boys and men, and sometimes boys and men from Georgia (a Republic in the Soviet Union, located in the Caucasus), had the fist name David. The Georgian boys and men, however, looked distinctly different, so, hearing that my first name is David, the women had no doubts that I was a Jew.

That was, as far as I remember, the first time in my life that I encountered a manifestation of anti-semitism. I do not think that I knew this word, anti-semitism, then, but I saw the ugly face of this monster.

End of the War

In the spring of 1945, the war between Germany and the Soviet Union was coming to the end. My mother, exhausted by the difficulties of the war-time, became ill. She spent some time in the hospital, where doctors tried different medications, but none of them worked. The doctors then came to the conclusion that in order to survive, my mother needed a radical change in her life. They sent a telegram to my father's superiors in the army, explaining the situation, and asking that he be given one month to spend at home, with his family.

The war just ended. My father, then a lieutenant and decorated for bravery, was immediately given permission to spend one month with his family. He came home sometime in May of 1945, in his military uniform, with a handgun. I did not remember my father at all. I was only four-and-a-half years old when the war parted us. He could not recognize me now. At the moment he came, I was playing with one of my class-mates. We both were skinny from lack of food. Maybe because of that, looked alike. "Manechka," asked my father (he always called my mother Manechka - a tender name for Maria), "which one is our son?"

Being a boy, I was interested in my father's handgun. It was a trophy German pistol of a distinctive design. Father called it "Parabellum." Father removed cartridges from the pistol, and I then was allowed to take the pistol in my hands. I tried to cock it but could not. There was not enough strength in my hands for that. The pistol belonged to the army. Father was issued it to use as his side-arm. After Father left for the army again, I never saw that kind of pistol for about forty-five years.

In 1990, I suddenly felt the urge to find out what exactly was that pistol my father came with in 1945. I talked with people in a Fargo store which sold guns. I described the pistol and was immediately told that that pistol was "Luger." And yes, that was the famous Luger Pistole Parabellum P08, Georg Luger's Masterpiece!

Why - after forty-five years - I suddenly felt the urge to find out more about that pistol - I do not know. That is something from the field of Psychology, I think, and I am not a psychologist ...

At the time my father came to spend one month with us, I was finishing the second grade. There was not enough paper to write homework, and I used small sheets of paper which we had from the pre-war time. One side of these sheets was filled with problems for math tests written in my father's handwriting, but the other side was blank, and I used that side for my homework. Looking through his pre-war test problems (or maybe he just wanted to know what we were doing in school), Father discovered that my teacher had explained to us that

$$zero \times one = zero \; , \quad but \quad one \times zero = one \; !$$

Father had to go to my school and to explain to my teacher (a young woman) that unity multiplied by zero is also zero. Why did she believe otherwise, I have no idea!

The war was behind, and we - my mother, my father, and I - were all alive. Without doubt, our survival in 1941, when the war started, was due to our move in 1939 from Kamenets-Podolsk to Moscow.

The Jews of Kamenets-Podolsk were killed by Germans on August 27 and 28 in 1941. In fact, twenty three thousand six hundred (23600) Jews were killed during those two days in the area of Kamenets-Podolsk. Of them, eighteen thousand (18000) were the Jewish deportees from Hungary (which declared war on the Soviet Union on June 27, 1941), and the rest were the local Jews.

This was "the first large-scale mass murder in pursuit of the 'Final Solution'" (United States Holocaust Memorial Museum. "Kamenets-Podolsk." Holocaust Encyclopedia. www.ushmm.org/wlc/en/article.php?ModuleId=10005442. Accessed on 1 December 2017).

My Father Returns Home from the Army

After the war, my father was offered a chance to stay in the army as a professional officer, in artillery. He did not want that. He wanted to return to his civilian life. In January of 1946, my father returned home. He was still in his uniform but without the badges of rank. And without the Parabellum, of course. According to the law, Father was entitled to get back his pre-war position, the position of the director of the school where we lived. However, he did not want to be an administrator anymore. (I think that he probably felt that his health suffered from the difficulties of the life at the front.) So he did not claim his pre-war job.

Instead, he started looking for a permanent position as a teacher of mathematics at a school. In the meantime, he had a couple of temporary jobs: teaching mathematics at the School of Militsia and teaching mathematics at a Vocational School. Then he was offered the position of the teacher of mathematics at a girls' school. He worked at that school for more than twenty years.

Father kept us - Mother and me - informed of what was going on in his professional life. We knew the names of some of his pupils. A few times, I was in his school and saw some of his pupils. I believe, I even talked with some of them on one or two occasions. At the same time, I do not remember my father ever talking with me about anything of a mathematical nature until I was at the very end of my school studies.

1953 - I Finish High School

I finished school in 1953. The duration of the school education in the Soviet Union was then ten years. The schools were open, as I have already mentioned before, Monday through Saturday, and the school year was from September 1 to June 23 (I think). There were ten (or twelve maybe) days of the winter recess. Whether or not there were any days of recess in the spring, I do not remember.

To graduate from school, every pupil had to pass examinations to receive the diploma. There were, as far as I remember, examinations in the Russian language and literature, in mathematics, physics, chemistry, and in a foreign language (English, in my case).

For the examination in mathematics, problems were prepared somewhere outside the schools, and they were given to the school directors in sealed envelopes. These envelopes were then opened on the day of examination, just before it (maybe thirty minutes before or so, to allow the teacher in charge to familiarize himself with the problems and to check them).

When the day of the examination in mathematics was close, my father told me that he wanted to spend some time with me and with two of my classmates, who were my friends, in order to prepare us better for the examination. Father could not know, of course, what problems would be given for that particular examination, but by that time he had been in charge of conducting such examinations in the schools where he had worked for probably a dozen years. So he had experience.

I have no recollection whatsoever of what mathematical questions my father touched during those three (or so) hours that he tutored us. I do remember, however, that two of us, one of my friends and I, got A's for that examination, and the third one got B. That friend who got A told me later that it was my father's choice of subjects and explanations that helped him to get his A.

I have to say that in addition to the excellent knowledge of mathematics and considerable experience, my father also had a natural ability to explain things extremely well - clearly, precisely, and concisely. I believe that in his district

(Moscow was divided in several districts) my father was regarded as the best school teacher of mathematics.

Father told me that he inherited his mathematical abilities from his mother, my grandmother Enia. She never studied any algebra but discovered some pieces of that discipline by herself, and used them in order to more efficiently operate the store (which my father's parents owned).

1953 Was the Most Difficult Year for a Jew To Be Admitted to an Institution of Higher Education

In June of 1953, I graduated from school. The next step was to apply to an Institution of Higher Education for admission. Admission to all such institutions was by examination: one had to arrive, in person, at the institution of his choice and take the entrance examination.

There was one exception, however, for people who had graduated from schools with what was called "medal." Those were the best achievers according to the results of the school-leaving examinations and to the school records, combined. Such people still had to arrive, in person, at the institution of their choices, but no entrance examination was given to them. Instead, they were interviewed and admitted.

And I did have a medal.

Now, in the Soviet Union the best Institutions of Higher Education were located in the big cities: in Moscow, in Leningrad, in Kiev, etc., and the graduates of the Moscow schools usually continued their education in Moscow, at one of the (numerous) Institutes or at the Moscow State University. So in theory everything should have been very simple for me. I had only to decide on the institution of my choice, in Moscow, to come in person, to submit my documents, to be interviewed and admitted. This should have been the end of story.

In reality, however, everything was not that simple. For me, a Jew that is. I could, of course, choose any institution in Moscow where I would want to become a student. I could come, and I could submit my documents. And they would, of course, talk with me. And then, if they had the directives not to admit Jews, or if they simply were not willing to admit Jews, they would turn me down. They did not have, according to the law, the right to do that. But they did it, and everybody who was a Jew knew that.

The year 1953 was an especially difficult year, the worst year ever, for somebody who was a Jew to try to get admitted to an Institution of Higher Education. "On January 13, 1953, some of the most prestigious and prominent doctors in the USSR were accused of taking part in a vast plot to poison members of the top Soviet political and military leadership." (Wikipedia, the Free Encyclopedia; http://en.wikipedia.org; Doctors' plot.) With the exception of two, all the accused doctors were Jewish.

In March of 1953, Stalin died. In April of 1953, the authorities admitted that the so-called Delo Vrachei (Doctors' plot) was fabricated. But anti-semitism continued to be at its highest peak through 1953 in the USSR. Still, I had to choose a future profession for myself and to try to get admitted to study that profession.

Until I was fifteen, I had liked all the subjects we studied in school more or less equally. However, since I reached fifteen, I felt that I liked mathematics more than any other subject. I saw only two choices for the direction of my studies. Either to study a branch of engineering where mathematics would be of considerable importance or to study mathematics itself and to become a mathematician.

To study any branch of engineering, I would need to master, among other subjects, engineering drawing. My father worried that I would not be able to do that: sometime in the last (10th) grade of school, my teacher of drawing talked with my father and told him that I had the lowest abilities in drawing of all the pupils of my class. I myself did not worry about that at all. I simply did not think of that.

To study mathematics as a profession, in Moscow, at that time, there were only four places from which a graduate of school could choose: the Moscow State University, the Moscow State Pedagogical Institute, and a couple of (everybody believed) semi-classified Institutes (the Moscow Institute of Engineering Physics and the Moscow Physico-Technical Institute).

The Moscow State University was the best university in the USSR, but for me, a Jew, to try to get admitted to that university in 1953 was absolutely hopeless; I did not even try. The two semi-clasified Institutes were also excellent places to study, but again, being a Jew, they were not open for me. The Pedagogical Institute - I could try ...

No matter where I would want to apply, there was one more obstacle which had to be overcome. It turned out that there existed a law that in order to become a student at an Institution of Higher Education, one had to be seventeen years of age or older. At my then age sixteen-and-a-half, I needed special permission, in writing, from the Ministry of Higher Education. Without such a permission, no Institution of Higher Education would accept my documents for consideration.

My father went to the Ministry of Higher Education to obtain the necessary permission for me. There he talked with some bureaucrat, who told him that in order to become a student, I should wait for one year. (The institutes and the universities were on the semester system, but admission was only once a year, from the beginning of the first semester.)

"And what is my son going to do during that year?" asked my father. "Oh," answered the bureaucrat, "your son could graze cows during that year." (There were, of course, no cows to graze and no pastures in the city of Moscow. He was not only a bureaucrat but an anti-semite.) Father had to talk with the bureaucrat's superior, and finally the necessary written permission for me was given.

I submitted my documents to the Bauman Moscow Higher Technical School, to become a student at the Fakul'tet (College) of Precision Mechanics. (The names of fakul'tets at that institution changed since that time, so I can not be sure that Precision Mechanics was the exact name of that fakul'tet.)

That School (also called then the Baumanskii Institute, and currently named the Bauman Moscow State Technical University), founded in 1830, had the reputation of being the best engineering institution of higher education in the entire Soviet Union. It was as highly regarded in the USSR as, for example, the Massachussets Institute of Technology (MIT) is regarded in the USA.

I was not admitted to the Bauman Moscow Higher Technical School. They had no right to say no to me, but I was a Jew, and they turned me down.

I then applied to the Moscow State Pedagogical Institute,

with a view to study mathematics (and if not, then physics). I was not accepted into the Moscow State Pedagogical Institute either. I was a Jew, and they rejected me.

I believe I visited some other Institutes at that time, but which ones - I do not remember. In each place I tried to talk with the fellow Jews, who were in the same situation I was.

Somebody, somewhere, told me that the Moscow Automobile and Road-Construction Institute was a place where a Jew like me could get admitted. I went immediately to that Institute and familiarized myself with the list of their specialties of study. I chose a specialty to study, but was told that that specialty was already not available and was offered to apply to study a different specialty, namely the specialty of the road-building machines (or so it was called).

I already knew that what I wanted did not matter, but only what "they" wanted. So I applied to study the road-building machines. I was admitted on the spot. Nobody even talked with me about anything. They just took my documents and told me, "You are admitted." Maybe they even gave me a letter stating that I was admitted before I left.

Until I came home, my parents knew nothing about what happened that day. We did not have a telephone in our apartment then, and I was unable to seek advice of my parents on the matter of that application. My parents did not like the specialty of the road-building machines as a future specialty for me. Frankly, I did not like it either.

Remark. *On the subject of the discrimination against Jews in the USSR, the reader is referred to the section* On the Discrimination Against Jews in the USSR *in Chapter 6 of the book.*

I Am Admitted To Study Naval Architecture (Shipbuilding)

We all decided that I had to take my documents back from the Automobile and Road-Construction Institute and to apply to the place of which I was already thinking for some time: the Fakul'tet (College) of Shipbuilding of the Moscow Technical Institute of the Fish Industry and Economy. At that fakul'tet, one could study shipbuilding (naval architecture), and, as a result of studies, the title of Naval Architect would be conferred on that person.

The perspective of becoming Naval Architect seemed attractive to me, and I also thought that in that profession I would be able to use a lot of mathematics. My parents also liked the idea of me applying to that fakul'tet.

At the Moscow Technical Institute of the Fish Industry and Economy (founded in 1930; in abbreviation: Mosrybvtuz), my application was treated with respect. I was interviewed by the Rector (Head) of the Institute himself. We talked - just the two of us - in his office.

That Professor (his name I do not remember) asked me about the main facts of my life and also why did I want to study shipbuilding. Then he warned me that the profession of Naval Architect is a difficult one to study and that the course of studies is the longest from what they had. I told him that I like difficult and unusual tasks (that quality, by the way, I inherited from my mother). That was the end of the interview; I was admitted!

During the interview with the Rector, my father and mother were waiting for me, on a bench, in front of the building of the Institute. When I appeared from the building and told my parents that I was admitted, they were happy: from the places which were available to me, I was admitted to a place which we - all three of us - liked. I was happy too.

The academic year at the Institute was from September 1 to June 23, with a two-weeks recess between semesters. Whether or not there was a spring break, I do not remember. The duration of the course for my specialization was officially five-and-a-half years. In reality, however, the duration of the course was a little longer than that. The timetable was prescribed by the Government, and, at least in my case, it took approximately five and two-thirds of the academic year (from the day I entered the Institute to the day I defended my Diploma Project) to finish the program.

The first five years were the years of classes, and the time for the Diploma Project was in the sixth year. The Institute worked six days per week, Monday through Saturday. Attendance at classes was mandatory, and, in my estimation, I had to be in class approximately thirty three hours per week in the first (two? three?) years of studies.

In summers, when the academic year was finished, we had the so-called Practices (Internships). Those we had after the second, third, fourth, and fifth academic years, and they were at Shipyards or at Ship Design Bureaus. One was the Sailing Practice, on a ship, at sea.

The courses to study, their contents, and their succession - all was prescribed by the Government. We studied a wide variety of courses, including the courses in Higher Mathematics, of course.

Remark. *The system of the Higher Education in the USSR,* *which was different from the system of the Higher Education in the USA, is described in the section* Higher Education in the USSR *in Chapter 6 of the book.*

I Want To Learn More Mathematics

At a certain moment, I realized that I wanted to learn much more mathematics than we studied. Here is how that happened. I took from the Library of the Institute a book on the theory of ocean waves and decided to study it on my own. I was able to master the first fifty or so pages of that book, but after that, I came across some mathematical equation where even the mathematical notations were unfamiliar to me. I was unable to read the book any further and returned it to the library.

After that, I tried to study some additional mathematics on my own, but after a couple of books, I realized that I really did not know what mathematics subject (or subjects) would be most expedient for me to study in addition to what we studied in classes. I then decided to go to the Chair of the Department of Higher Mathematics of the Institute, Professor Maksim Isidorovich Gurevich, and to talk with him.

Professor M.I. Gurevich was not the person who lectured us on mathematics. A woman, Dotsent (Associate Professor), her name I do not remember, was the one. But on a few occasions, when she was out of town (or ill maybe), he came to lecture us, and that is how I knew of him.

Professor Gurevich told me that a proper subject for me to study (in addition to what we studied in classes) would be the Theory of Functions of a Complex Variable. He told me that that was a very important mathematical discipline, very useful in applications (to hydrodynamics, for example).

I thanked the Professor and left. That is how my interest in Complex Variables started. I was then, I think, about eighteen. My next conversation with Professor Gurevich took place several years later, when I was twenty-six.

For a period of time, my attempts at mastering the discipline of Complex Variables were not that successful. I took one book on the subject but read only part of it. I took another book, and that one I studied from cover to cover. When I finished studying that book, I was under the impression that I had mastered the subject of Complex Variables. But I hadn't! I was not solving problems, just studying the theory. So I did not yet have the practical knowledge of the subject of Complex Variables.

My Father's Advice Was Invaluable to Me

I then talked with my father. I described to him my attempts at self-study of mathematics, Complex Variables in particular. I told him that my goal was to learn a lot of mathematics, to know it in the amount and on the level of the mathematicians who graduate from, for example, the Moscow State University. Father told me that I should take a textbook on the Differential and Integral Calculuses for the students of universities majoring in mathematics and to master that textbook first.

My father's advice was invaluable to me. I did as he suggested and later was able to build on that foundation, studying one mathematical subject after another without hindrance.

The textbook on the Differential and Integral Calculuses which I have chosen was huge (in three volumes, more than 2000 pages total), had a lot of solved examples, and I also solved a big number of problems when studying that textbook. It took a considerable amount of time to master that course, but when I finished it, I felt that I was prepared extremely well in the fields of the Differential and Integral Calculuses, both from the point of view of theory and from the point of view of practice.

I Graduated, I Am a Naval Architect. But Being a Jew, the Prestigious Research Institute TsAGI Did Not Hire Me

My education at the Shipbuilding Fakul'tet of the Mosrybvtuz came to its end in the middle of March of 1959, when I defended my Diploma Project. Mosrybvtuz gave us, students who were studying Naval Architecture, an excellent fundamental engineering education.

One of my Professors, who was a specialist in the field of hydrodynamics, worked at TsAGI (Central Aerohydrodynamics Institute) in Moscow; that Professor taught at Mosrybvtuz part-time. He wanted me to work at his unit at TsAGI, and he invited me to apply for the position they had open. The name of that Professor was Leonid Abramovich Epshtein.

TsAGI was a very prestigious research institution, one of the best places in the USSR to conduct research in the field of Naval Hydrodynamics. That was also a classified institution. I did apply but was not hired: I was a Jew, and that was the USSR of 1958-1959.

I Am Required To Study Welding Engineering

My professional future depended at that moment on the Government. According to the law, the Government had the right to send me to work for three years at any place in the Soviet Union where specialists of my profile were needed. And that is what I expected to happen to me.

The Government, however, had a different plan for us, fifty (or so) young specialists who graduated that year from the Fakul'tet of Shipbuilding of my Institute with the title of Naval Architect. The Government, at that time, had a need for engineers in the field of welding. So the Government decided to send us to study, for a period of several months, welding engineering, with a view to employ us, after that, in the field of welding. I had no desire to study welding engineering and to work in that field, but I had no choice.

It turned out that the Government had a certain plan for the Moscow Technical Institute of the Fish Industry and Economy too. In 1959, the Institute was transferred from Moscow to the city of Kaliningrad.

Kaliningrad was previously called Konigsberg, and before the Second World War it belonged to Germany. After the war, the land where Konigsberg was located, called East Prussia, was divided between the USSR and Poland. Konigsberg became the city in the USSR.

I knew of that city in particular from what my father told my mother and me about the events of the war in which he participated. The Army to which my father's artillery unit belonged finished the war at Konigsberg.

Incidentally, Konigsberg was the city where the famous mathematician Karl Gustav Jacobi (1804-1851) lived and worked (at the University of Konigsberg, from 1826 to 1844). Running many steps forward, I shall mention here that one of the mathematics subjects of my research in Fargo, North Dakota, was Elliptic Functions, and that is the area to which Jacobi made fundamental contributions. His work "Fundamenta Nova Theoriae Functionum Ellipticarum" was published in 1829, three years after Jacobi moved (from Berlin) to Konigsberg.

Konigsberg was renamed Kaliningrad in 1946. Kaliningrad was one of the cities in the USSR where my summer Practices (Internships) took me. I was in Kaliningrad in 1958, during my Pre-Diploma Practice. I remember one place in the city where, I was told, the building of a theatre stood before the war. There were pieces of brick, and maybe some brick walls at that place, nothing else. Or - at least that is how I see that place in my memory. And that was thirteen years after the war ended. The city was probably damaged severely during the war.

When Mosrybvtuz was transferred to Kaliningrad, the name of the Institute was changed. Later, the Institute became a University. Today it is the Kaliningrad State Technical University. The Fakul'tet (College) where I studied is called the Shipbuilding and Power Engineering Fakul'tet today (2018).

Well, as I mentioned, I had no desire to study welding engineering (in 1959). But at least the place where the Government was sending us to study that specialty was one of the best places (if not the best place) to study it: the Bauman Moscow Higher Technical School.

What an irony of fate! In 1953, that School did not admit me as a student: I was a Jew. In 1959, I was obligated to go and to study at that School, although I did not really want to study what they were going to teach me. The duration of those studies was seven and one-third months, non-stop, without any breaks. (That was about 80% of the duration of the academic year in the USSR, and amounts to about one full academic year here, at the North Dakota State University, in Fargo, ND.)

I Work as an Engineer; I Continue My Self-Studies of Mathematics

By December 1, 1959, my studies of welding engineering at the Baumanskii Institute were finished, and in early 1960, I started working life as an engineer.

Before and during the time that I studied welding engineering, and in the later years, when I was working as an engineer, my main interest was in the continuation of my self-studies of mathematics. In that area, after the Differential and Integral Calculuses, I returned to the subject of Complex Variables. I say returned, since I had already tried to study that subject but was not satisfied with the results of my previous studies of it.

This time, thanks to the advice of my father to first study the Differential and Integral Calculuses in the proper amount and on the proper level, I was very well prepared to master the subject of Complex Variables.

Complex Variables, or Complex Analysis, as it is also called, is one of the cornerstones of mathematics, and that subject was covered by me, this time, very thoroughly. I used several books (or portions of books) to study the foundations of the theory of Complex Variables and the applications of that theory.

Since Complex Analysis is used in a number of other branches of mathematics, thorough knowledge of that subject helped me eventually in my studies of those branches (in the studies of Functional Analysis, for example, in the studies of Elliptic Functions, in the studies of Bessel functions, etc.).

After the Years of Self-Studies of Mathematics, My Main Goal Is To Do Research

I studied many mathematical subjects after Complex Analysis. In 1963, when I was twenty six years old, I knew that I was prepared - broadly and deeply - in the field of Mathematics. Also, having by that time considerable experience in acquiring mathematical knowledge, I had no doubts that I would be able to learn, if it would become necessary in the future, additional mathematical disciplines too. I wanted then to do research.

I have already tried my hand at the theoretical research, somewhat. When I was a student at Mosrybvtuz, our Professor of Structural Mechanics, A.I. Segal', erudite in his field, posted a list of subjects for us, students, to explore. I volunteered for one of those subjects, and later I made a presentation on the subject. The presentation was intended for students, but two of our Professors, A.I. Segal' and our Professor of Theoretical Mechanics (his name I do not remember), were present.

The presentation was based on a paper published by Professor A.I. Segal' earlier. Reading the paper and thinking of the subject, I discovered some new details which were not in the paper, and I included them in my presentation. I did not tell the audience that these details were discovered by me though.

I have to say that when I volunteered to explore the subject of the presentation, I just took a copy of Professor Segal's paper and left. After a period of time, I came and told the Professor that I was ready to make the presentation. And on the day and time specified, I made the presentation. I never spoke with the Professor about the subject of the presentation, so he learned of my small findings just from the presentation itself.

After I finished the presentation, Professor Segal' came to the blackboard and told the audience that, although the presentation was based on his paper, there were some new things in the presentation which were not contained in his paper, and which I discovered on my own. And he listed those things and explained what exactly they were.

That was the first time that somebody - namely, one of my Professors, whom I highly respected, and whose lectures and the subject, theoretical in nature, I liked very much - recognized and acknowledged my creative abilities in theoretical research. I was eighteen (or nineteen) then. That was a big encouragement for me. I never forgot it.

Another time when I did a piece of research work, both theoretical and experimental in this case, was during my first engineering job. That was a study of a pneumatic-drive-hydraulic-brake system of a large welding machine. I made some reasonable engineering (or physical) assumptions about the hydraulic brake, then wrote the equation of motion (I think, I do not remember any details, that was long time ago), used integration maybe, and after I received the results, represented them graphically in the form of a nomogram.

Nomography was a branch of mathematics which I have mastered on my own when I was a student studying Naval Architecture. That was before I came to Professor M.I. Gurevich to ask for his advice on what mathematical subject would be most proper for me to study (in addition to what we studied in classes). My study of nomography paid off, and the nomogram which I constructed worked perfectly well. This, however, was the only time in my life that I had to construct a nomogram. My study of nomography served me but was of importance to me for only relatively short period of time.

To the contrary, my study of Complex Variables, which I initiated on the advice of Professor M.I. Gurevich, has served me for the duration of the lifetime. One can see that when reading most of my published articles or my books References [5], [6].

So in 1963 my main goal was to do research. Research in which mathematics would be of vital, central importance. And to eventually write my Kandidat Nauk Dissertation (Ph.D. Dissertation) on the basis of that research. And when the Dissertation was ready, to defend it.

I Am Admitted to Aspirantura (Ph.D. Program)

There were two ways to accomplish that task. One was to enter Aspirantura as a day-time, full-time Aspirant (as it was and is today called). Another one was to find a job where doing research of the kind I wanted to do would be my duties (or a considerable part of my duties) and to then enter Aspirantura as an extramural Aspirant.

I did not think that I would have had difficulties in entering Aspirantura or in finding a proper research job if I were not a Jew. Being a Jew, as usual, complicated things enormously.

Nevertheless, I had to try. I was then married, and we had a four-year-old daughter. The family needed money to live, of course, so my first thought was to find a proper research job and to enter Aspirantura extramurally. I tried to find such a job, but I couldn't.

   Then, one day somebody told me that there was a vacant position of Assistant Professor at the Department of Theoretical Mechanics of the Moscow Institute of Engineers of Railway Transport (acronym: MIIT). And I was told that if I were interested in the position, I had to call the Chair of that Department, Professor Maksim Isidorovich Gurevich.

   Yes, that was the same Professor Gurevich who previously was the Chair of the Department of Higher Mathematics at the Institute where I studied Naval Architecture, and who, eight (or so) years earlier, gave me a piece of advice to study Complex Variables! When that Instutute was transferred to Kaliningrad, Professor Gurevich stayed in Moscow, and now he was working at MIIT.

   I called Professor Gurevich, told him who I was, and that I was interested in the position of Assistant Professor which they had open. I also reminded him that years ago I came to him to ask for a piece of advice on what mathematical discipline to choose for self-study.

   Professor Gurevich did not remember me at all. But he invited me to come to the place where he lived to talk. When I came, the first thing Professor wanted to find out was what was my nationality by my passport? When I told him that by my passport my nationality was a Jew, he told me openly that, in this case, the administration of the Institute, MIIT, would not allow him to hire me.

   And then he asked me why I did want the position of Assistant Professor at their Department. In response, I explained to him that what I really wanted was to do research, of the kind where mathematics would be of central importance. And that I was well-prepared in the field of mathematics by years of self-studies. And that if I worked at a place like his Department, I would then be among scientists, people doing research, etc.

The Professor told me that if doing research was what I really wanted, then I should try to enter their Aspirantura. They had a vacancy, and if I were to take the entrance examinations and get good enough grades, I may become his Aspirant. And he explained that at their Institute, MIIT, the Pro-Rector (Vice Rector, Vice Head of the Institute) in charge of Research and Aspirantura was Armenian by nationality. Professor Gurevich (who was a Jew himself) thought that Armenians were friendly to us, Jews, and he thought that that Pro-Rector would not be against me becoming an Aspirant at MIIT.

If admitted to Aspirantura, I would have three years - for studies, research, and for the preparation of the Kandidat Nauk Dissertation, three years free of any other duties. The Government was paying a stipend to Aspirants, every month, for thirty six months in a row. That stipend was sizeably smaller than my then salary of engineer, but still my family could manage.

I came to the Personnel Department of MIIT to take the necessary forms to fill in. They were not eager, however, to give me the forms. A woman from the Personnel Department told me that the vacancy for Professor Gurevich's Aspirant was for somebody who was educated at the Mekhanico-Mathematical Fakul'tet of the Moscow State University or had an equivalent education in the field of mathematics. And according to my documents, I was educated as an engineer, not as a mathematician.

Professor Gurevich then offered a solution: he would give me a certain scientific book and would ask me to write an essay on a certain topic from that book. That would allow him to determine what was my level of preparation in mathematics.

The book which he gave me was on the subject of hydrodynamics and was based on mathematics. I wrote an essay, where some parts of the discussion were new things which I was able to do due to my knowledge of the Theory of Singular Integral Equations, one of the subjects which I had mastered in the course of my self-studies of mathematics.

Having read that essay, Professor Gurevich came to the conclusion that I was very well prepared mathematically to become his Aspirant. He told that to me, and he probably told that to the Personnel Department too, since the necessary forms were then given to me. I filled in and submitted the forms, took the necessary examinations, got all A's, and was admitted to Aspirantura of MIIT. That happened in 1963. I was happy, and my parents were happy too.

Remark. *The meaning of the word* Nationality *in the USSR was different from the meaning of the same word in the USA. That difference is explained in the section* Meaning of the Word Nationality *in Chapter 6 of the book.*

Years at Aspirantura

MIIT, where I spent the next three years of my life, from October 1963 to October 1966, was founded in 1896. Today this institution is called the Moscow State University of Railway Engineering.

My Rukovoditel' at Aspirantura (Leading Professor; in the USA: Ph.D. Adviser), Professor M.I. Gurevich (1909-1975), was a mathematician educated at the Moscow State University. By experience, he was an applied mathematician, working mainly in the fields of Hydrodynamics, Aerodynamics, and Acoustics.

He originally worked at TsAGI. TsAGI, as I have already mentioned above, was a classified institution. Every morning, coming to work, Dr. Gurevich had to show a guard his pass - to be let in. One morning - in 1949 (I think) that happened - when he, as usual, showed his pass to a guard, the guard looked at some list, took the pass away, and told Dr. Gurevich, "You are not employed by TsAGI anymore." Well, that was the Soviet Union of 1949, and Dr. M.I. Gurevich was a Jew.

His attempts to find a job were unsuccessful until 1951, when he finally found employment with the Moscow Technical Institute of the Fish Industry and Economy (where I first met him).

In 1961, Professor Gurevich published (in Moscow, in the Russian language) a book on the Theory of Jets in Ideal Fluids Ref. [2]. In 1964, that book was awarded a Prize - from the Academy of Sciences of the USSR (S.A. Chaplygin's Prize). That book was also translated into English. Two different translations of the book were made, and two different English versions of the book were published: one in the USA, in 1965, by Academic Press Ref. [3], and another one in England, in 1966, by Pergamon Press Ref. [4]. That was very unusual and testified to the high virtues of the book.

By the way, Maksim Isidorovich (that is how Professor Gurevich was usually addressed in everyday life) told me that it took him eight years to write that book.

Well, I became Professor Gurevich's Aspirant in October of 1963, and the first thing Professor asked me to do was to study a couple of chapters of a book on hydrodynamics and aerodynamics (as his book, that was an applied-mathematical book, with the subjects of applications being hydrodynamics and aerodynamics). I took the book, came home, and started working on those chapters. For a period of a month after that, I disappeared from the field of vision of Professor Gurevich.

I have to explain that at Aspirantura I only had to attend classes on two subjects, and each class for a limited period of time. The first subject was the English language, and the second one was the so-called Marxist-Lenin Philosophy. Both were mandatory courses. Everything else was studied by self-studies.

Reading the chapters which I had to read, I realized that I could do a piece of research on a particular subject discussed in one of those chapters, and I did it. All this took me one month, during which I never came to see my Professor. Then, suddenly, the Secretary of our Department called me. Professor Gurevich wanted to know if I was at Aspirantura, or did I drop out?

I was very surprised. "Why," I asked, "does the Professor think that I maybe dropped out of Aspirantura?" "Oh," she said, "because Aspirants always come and ask the Professor questions, and you never came and never asked any questions!" "Well," I said, "I was not coming because I had no questions to ask, that is why!" "Anyway," she said, "Professor asks you to come."

I came and, after a short converstion, handed the

Professor the piece of research I prepared. He took it home to read. Next time I saw Maksim Isidorovich, he told me: "I asked you to study the chapters in the book, but you not only studied them but went forward and did a piece of research where new things are done. I have no reasons to worry about your success at Aspirantura anymore. You will be successful."

The three years at Aspirantura were filled with studies and research. I did not allow myself any vacations during those three years. One time, however, Maksim Isidorovich insisted that I would go to the Tomsk State University, in Tomsk, to make a presentation at the Third Siberian Conference on Mathematics and Mechanics. To get to Tomsk and back, by train, took me probably six or seven days. I had a mathematical book with me on the train, and I was studying it though. I did not want to lose any time.

At the end of my third year at Aspirantura, I had my Dissertation ready - written, typed, and bound. In accordance with the rules which existed then in the Soviet Union, a Disseration could not be defended at the Institution where it was written (prepared). That is, I had to submit my Dissertation for defense to an Institution different from MIIT.

I Am Kandidat of Physico-Mathematical Sciences (Ph.D., in Physico-Mathematical Sciences)

I submitted my Dissertation to the Institute for the Problems of Mechanics of the Academy of Sciences of the USSR. That was a very prestigious Research Institution, and proper for defense of my Dissertation.

The Dissertation was defended by me in March of 1967. The Scientific Council of the Institute for the Problems of

Mechanics consisted of thirty members; twenty five of them were present at my defense. The voting was by secret ballot, and of twenty five votes, twenty five were for that the degree of Kandidat Nauk would be conferred on me, zero against.

It was required in the Soviet Union that after the defense all the defended Dissertations were sent to a Govermental Agency called The Higher Attestation Commission. The Higher Attestation Commission had the right to affirm - or not to affirm - the results of the defense. Only that Commission had the right to award the Kandidat Nauk Degree; the Institution where the Dissertation was defended could only recommend awarding the degree.

The results of my defense were affirmed, and I then received the Diploma of Kandidat of Physico-Mathematical Sciences (Kandidat Nauk, equivalent to Ph.D., in Physico-Mathematical Sciences), in 1967.

My parents, who saw how I worked long years, acquiring mathematical knowledge first, and then, at Aspirantura, continuing that process and doing research, were happy for me.

About My Research During the Years of Aspirantura

In the years of my self-studies of Mathematics, my main goal was to acquire broad and deep mathematical knowledge, with a view to later use that knowledge in solving problems of the Natural Sciences and Engineering.

My reseach during the years of Aspirantura was in the area of the Jet Flows, specifically - in the area of the Theory of Jets in Ideal Fluids.

Specialists of different professions have worked in the field of the Jet Flows. According to Professor Garrett Birkhoff (1911-1996) of the Mathematics Department of Harvard University and to E.H. Zarantonello (1918-2010), mathematician of Universidad Nacional de Cuyo Mendoza, Argentina, authors of the book "Jets, Wakes, and Cavities" Ref. [1], that is what those specialists have done in that field:

"Classical applied mathematicians have treated in detail many special flows ... . Pure mathematicians have stressed general aspects of 'ideal' fluid theory, such as questions of existence and uniquiness, almost exclusively. Specialists in modern fluid dynamics, guided by intuition and fragmentary reasoning, have found various relationships of great importance for engineering applications ... . Finally, physicists have established many striking effects under controlled laboratory conditions ... " Ref. [1, page v].

In my Aspirantura years, I did in the Theory of Jets in Ideal Fluids what classical applied mathematicians do in that field: treated in detail a number of special flows.

I have to say that the Theory of Jets in Ideal Fluids is mostly an applied-mathematical subject. In particular, one of the translations of the book on the Theory of Jets in Ideal Fluids by M.I. Gurevich, Ref. [4], mentioned above, was published by Pergamon Press as a part of the International Series of Monographs in Pure and Applied Mathematics.

After Aspirantura

From the end of 1966 and until the end of 1971, I worked at the Institute for the Problems of Mechanics, in the Department of the Theory of Elasticity of that Institute.

I have three articles published - on the subject of vibrations of elastic bodies, which were written in those years or later. And I had some amount of material prepared for study of vibrations of elastic membranes, as a result of work in those years. However, when I left the Soviet Union (later), I was not allowed to take this material with me. In the USA, I tried, at some moment, to return to this subject of research but actually never restored the material which I had on this subject in the USSR. Unfortunately, I have to say ...

After the years at the Institute for the Problems of Mechanics, I returned to the research in the field of Hydrodynamics.

TsAGI Does Not Hire Me Again. This Time, I Knew Exactly Why: the KGB Did Not Allow To Hire Me

When I was working at the Institute for the Problems of Mechanics, at a certain moment it looked like I would be offered a job at TsAGI (Central Aerohydrodynamics Institute). At TsAGI, both my knowledge and my skills in the field of Mathematics and my knowledge of Naval Architecture could have been utilized together.

As I have already mentioned above, after I finished my Naval Architecture education, one of my professors, L.A. Epshtein, invited me to work in his laboratory at TsAGI. However, TsAGI did not hire me then.

This time I was invited to make a presentation at TsAGI, with a view to offer me a job at TsAGI after that. I made the presentation but was not offered the job. This-time, I knew exactly why.

Professor Epshtein was still working at TsAGI at that time, and he attended my presentation in question. He knew well a woman from the Personnel Department of TsAGI. She used to work in his laboratory as a technician. He asked that woman why I was not offered a job at TsAGI. The woman told him that the Personnel Department of TsAGI could not offer a job to anybody without first asking the KGB. And, she told him, the KGB did not give them the permission to hire me. End of story.

The KGB was, of course, the secret police in the Soviet Union, and they were also involved in the espionage abroad.

After the Institute for the Problems of Mechanics

As I mentioned above, after the Institute for the Problems of Mechanics, I returned in my research to the field of Hydrodynamics.

I worked at two Research and Development (R&D) Institutes during those years. At one of them, my job was directly connected to the Theory of Jet Flows, at another one - it was not.

Between 1973 and 1976, I published six research articles with hydrodynamics being the subject of applications in them. The nature of my research continued to be mostly applied-mathematical. However, in a couple of those articles, some considerations were more of the kind pure mathematicians usually do in the field of the Theory of Jets in Ideal Fluids.

I Want To Leave the Soviet Union

I was born and raised in the USSR, and before my mother and I left that country, never was in any other country, even as a tourist.

Gradually, I came to the conclusion that it would be the right thing for me to leave the USSR. Since sometime in the early 1970s, for somebody who was a Jew that was not an impossible thing. The Soviet Government could give me the permission to leave, or they could deny me the permission to leave; in the latter case, my life in the Soviet Union would become very difficult.

Well, I could try, but there was one more obstacle: I was divorced, had a daughter, and according to the law, when the daughter was younger than eighteen, I needed, when applying for the exit visa, to have a letter from my former wife stating that she was not against me leaving the country. And my former wife did not want to give me such a letter. So I had to wait until my daughter is eighteen.

On the day my daughter was eighteen, I submitted my and my mother's applications for the exit visas. That was in the beginning of 1977. There were only two of us to apply as my father died in 1976. When I submitted our applications, the woman to whom I submitted them (in the organization named OVIR: Department of Visas and Registration) told me, "You also need a letter from your former wife." "Not today," I replied, "today my daughter is eighteen."

Chapter 2

In The USA

My Mother and I Leave the Soviet Union

In the summer of 1977, my mother and I left the Soviet Union. Aeroflot (USSR's Airlines) brought us to Vienna, Austria, and then, by train, we arrived at Rome, Italy. Waiting for the entrance visas to the USA, we lived in Italy for about three months.

We were given a small book in Italy, with the description of how our everyday life in the USA can be different from the life in the Soviet Union. I do not have that book today, and I remember not much of what was written in that book. One section from that book, however, was very helpful to me - the section with the description of the educational degrees in the USA and with the information to what degrees (in the USA) our degrees and diplomas from the Soviet Union are equivalent.

From that book, I learned that the highest educational degree in the USA is Ph.D., that my USSR's Kandidat Nauk degree is equivalent to USA's Ph.D., and that my Diploma of Engineer from the Soviet Union is equivalent to the Master's degree in the USA.

We were admitted to the United States as Jewish Refugees from the Soviet Union.

We Are in the USA

In the autumn of 1977, my mother and I arrived in the USA. We lived on the East Coast, and my main concern at that time was, of course, to find a job, anywhere in the United States.

That turned out to be a difficult task. Almost half of the research articles which I published in the Soviet Union (seven out of fifteen articles) were translated into English and published in the West too. But - personally I did not know any of the scientists in the USA.

Maksim Isidorovich Gurevich gave me the names and the addresses of two American scientists to contact if and when I arrived in the United States. One of these scientists was Professor Garrett Birkhoff, of the Mathematics Department of Harvard University, and another one was H. Cohen, who worked at the Thomas J. Watson Research Laboratory of IBM, and who, I believe, was in charge of all research projects of that Laboratory at that time.

I did send letters to both of them, but that did not help me to find a job. H. Cohen answered that he could not find a proper research project for me to work on, and Professor Birkhoff answered that he had several Ph.D. students, and he needed to help them to find jobs.

Temporary Jobs and the Beginning of My Research Activity in the USA

My first job in the USA was at a small Research and Development (R&D) Company on the East Coast. That job was offered to me as a temporary short-term job. My second job was at the Department of Mechanical

Engineering of Stevens Institute of Technology (in Hoboken, NJ), a temporary, one-year position.

My first article based on the research carried out by me in the United States was published in 1980, in the *Journal of Hydronautics*. That article was submitted by me from Stevens Institute of Technology, but the work itself was performed earlier, when I worked at the R&D Company. The *Journal of Hydronautics* is printed on the letter-size paper (8.5 inches x 11 inches), and the article in question was a short (about two pages) note.

After my job at Stevens ended, I looked for another job and continued doing research, writing and publishing articles based on that research.

My second article, submitted a few months after my job at Stevens ended, was based on the research done at Stevens, and it was published in 1982, in the *Journal of Ship Research*. This journal is also printed on the letter-size paper, and the article in question occupied twelve pages of the journal. Thus, that was an article of a rather good size.

Finding a job continued to be a difficult problem. Research jobs for me probably required security clearance. And not being a US citizen, I was not eligible to get such a clearance.

But - there was a hope. Time was going by, my mother and I needed to live in the United States five years in order to be eligible for the US Citizenship. Moreover, to submit our applications for the US Citizenship, we had to live in the USA four years and ten months. So four years and ten months after we arrived in the USA, we submitted our applications.

We Are the Naturalized Citizens of the USA, but I Am Not Given Security Clearance

In 1983, I became a Naturalized US Citizen; my mother became US citizen two years later. I still have those two American flags, of a small size, which we were given on the days we became US Citizens.

Now I could write in my resume: Citizen of the USA - since 1983.

Some time after I started sending resumes with this addition to it, I received a telephone call from a Company located in New Orleans, Louisiana. The Company was building Air-Cushion Vehicles for the US Navy. No wonder they were interested in me: a number of my publications were on the subject of the Jet Curtain of an Air-Cushion Vehicle.

I tried to recall the name of that company but could not. On the Internet, I found the name Textron Marine, in New Orleans, LA, and probably that was the name of the company.

The person who called told me that he was originally from England and was educated in England. He understood, he told me, that as he, I had received a fundamental European education and would be able to do whatever the company would need me to do (or something to that effect he told me).

I told him that I would not be able to name three references in the profession, to recommend me. "Somebody who publishes in the *Journal of Ship Research*," he replied, "does not need any additional recommendations." And he told me that the company would apply for the security clearance for me, and when the clearance was received, he would call me again.

Time passed, but he did not call. Finally, I called him myself. And then I learned the bitter news: the security clearance was not given to me. When President Reagan came to power, I was told, the rules for issuing the security clearances became more strict. And I had a daughter living, at that time, in the Soviet Union. That, as far as I understood, was the reason that the security clearance was not given to me.

About My Daughter

Yes, my daughter was living then in Moscow, USSR. Connections between me and my daughter were practically non-existent. Her mother and I were divorced, and when her mother remarried, she cut off any connections between my daughter and me and my mother and father. That happened when my daughter was about twelve-and-a-half years old, and since then, I did not see my daughter for about six years.

I knew, however, from one of my acquaintances, that after the high school my daughter became a student at the Moscow Institute of Civil Engineering. Before my mother and I left the Soviet Union, I came to the Institute and talked with my daughter. That was a short conversation during break between her two classes. I asked her in particular whether she wanted me to write letters to her from abroad. She answered, "No." That was in 1977, and my daughter was eighteen then.

Sometime in the early 1980s, when we lived on the East Coast of the United States, my mother decided to try to contact my daughter, her granddaughter. She wrote a letter to my daughter and sent it to a woman in Moscow whom my mother knew, asking that woman to contact my daughter and to hand her the letter. That woman met with my daughter and handed her the letter. However, nothing positive came out of that. My daughter told that woman that she would not answer the letter, and my mother, indeed, never received any letter from her granddaughter. My daughter was a young adult then, when she refused to answer the letter from her grandmother, my mother.

Thus, the connections between me and my daughter were practically non-existent. Besides, even if the connections between us were normal, I would never have allowed any harm to be done to my country, United States of America, because of these connections. But how could a person who had to make a decision about security clearance for me be sure of that? He probably simply followed the rules, and for that I can not blame him.

When I learned from the Textron Marine that I was not given the security clearance, I had tears in my eyes. They did not trust me in the USSR, and now they - although very different "they" - do not trust me here, in the United States!

After that experience with the Textron Marine, it became clear to me that my hopes that it would be easier for me to find a job in my new country after I became a Citizen (of the United States) - were just an illusion ...

Permanent Job for Me Is Found - at the North Dakota State University (NDSU), in Fargo, North Dakota

The third research article written by me in the United States was very large, twenty one letter-size pages. It was published in the *Journal of Ship Research* in the spring of

1985. And approximately at that time, the permanent job for me was found.

The job was found with the help of the immigrants from the Soviet Union. Somebody from that Russian-speaking community introduced me to somebody else. That person asked me to give him my published articles, and after that, he introduced me to somebody in the Department of Mathematics of the North Dakota State University (NDSU), in Fargo, North Dakota. I applied for the open position in the Department, was invited for the interview, and was hired, as Associate Professor of Mathematics.

My mother and I were happy. Finally, there was a place in the United States where I had the permanent job, and where we could live.

Working at NDSU

My job in the Department of Mathematics of NDSU required 60% teaching, 30% research, and 10% service. The academic year at NDSU was at that time divided into three quarters, and for the first two quarters of my first academic year, I had no time for research at all.

I have to explain that before NDSU I did teach mathematics in the USSR, but only occasionally. My main activity in the USSR, from the time of Aspirantura, was in the area of research, not in the area of teaching.

My philosophy with respect to my new job was very simple. I am a researcher, and I like to do research most. *However, in my new job, I have to earn the right to do research, by first teaching my students in the best way.* That was my philosophy, my attitude, and I believe I was right in that.

In order to deliver as perfect lectures as I could, I had to first prepare each of them in the best way. That was taking a very large amount of time for each lecture. However, after such preparations, I could, using my natural ability to teach (a gift for teaching inherited from my father), deliver clear, precise, and concise lectures - for the benefit of my students.

In the third quarter of my first academic year at NDSU, sometime in the spring of 1986, I was able to return to my research activity, to start my research at NDSU. In the subsequent years, the more courses I had already prepared the more time I was able to spend doing research.

And of course, there were summers, when I could do research without interruption. With one exception. In the summer of 1987, my mother insisted that I should interrupt my research activity and go with her to Israel. She wanted to see our relatives, some of whom she had never seen before, but we knew of them, and they knew of us, and some of whom she had not seen since the end of the Second World War. That trip to Israel took about three weeks.

My Mother Dies

I am glad that I did interrupt my research then and go to Israel with my mother. She could not go alone. Four months later, in December of 1987, my mother died.

My mother called my father and me - "boys." By the time I was born, my mother knew my father for about eleven years. After my father died, my mother lived for eleven more years, and then she died. As if she wanted to spend equal amount of time in this life with each of her boys, with my father, and with me ...

After my mother died, for some period of time I was almost not talking in classes. My lectures were very well prepared and all written, so I was simply writing out the material of my prepared lectures on blackboard. In March, I believe, when there was more sun, I started talking in classes again.

Students liked my teaching, and in 1988 I received the Outstanding Teacher Award from the Division of Mathematical Sciences (Mathematics, Computer Science, and Statistics Departments; thirty professors total) of the North Dakota State University. The Award was based on student nominations.

Tenure Consideration - for Me, at NDSU - Begins. The PT&E Committee Recommends Not To Grant Me Tenure

In 1990-1991 academic year, after five years of work at NDSU, the consideration for granting me tenure was taking place, and in November-December of 1990, the Promotion, Tenure, and Evaluation Committee (the PT&E Committee) of the College of Science and Mathematics of NDSU was considering my case.

By that time, I had accumulated a very large amount of research results obtained at NDSU. However, most of the results were not in the condition where they could have been submitted for publication. To bring these results to the ready-to-be-submitted-for-publication condition - I needed more time.

The matter was that the majority of the results in question, although they belonged to different mathematics subjects (complex variables, elliptic functions, integral equations), were based on similar ideas, and because of that, they were interconnected. This created the situation when I had to work at *all* these results simultaneously, preferably - until the point when *all* these results would be ready for submission, and to submit them for publication after that. And to reach that *all*-are-ready-for-submission point, I needed more time.

   Some of my research results, however, were not connected to other results; these results I could submit for publication, and I did it. Two research articles were submitted by me from NDSU. One of them has already been accepted for publication, and another one was under consideration in a journal - at the time when the PT&E Committee was considering me for tenure.

   At the time of my meeting with the PT&E Committee, I told them that during my work at NDSU my productivity in research was higher than when I was younger.

   I received a letter from the PT&E Committee. They recognized that I had achieved notable success in teaching. They recommended not to grant me tenure, because of my record in research at NDSU.

   Well, at that moment I could not expect that the PT&E Committee would recommend granting me tenure. A faculty from my Department (Mathematics Department of NDSU), who previously served on the PT&E Committee of the College of Science and Mathematics, and who, I am sure, knew the rules (because he served on that Committee), asked me several months earlier if I was going to apply for tenure? And when I answered "Yes", he told me that I would need two articles.

That is, from that information, I knew that one research article submitted from NDSU and accepted for publication would not be sufficient for obtaining tenure; I needed to have two such articles. And at that time, as I have mentioned above, I had only one research article accepted for publication; the second article was still under consideration. That was in November- December of 1990.

Good News: My Second Submitted from NDSU Research Article Is Highly Recommended for Publication

In February of 1991, I received good news about my second submitted from NDSU research article. It has been *highly recommended* for publication, subject to some editorial changes. Those editorial changes were simply improvements in the English language in some places of the article, suggested by the referee.

I did those improvements and sent the article to the editor of the journal. It was absolutely clear at that moment that my second research article would be accepted for publication, and thus, I would have two research articles submitted from NDSU and accepted for publication. Together with my *notable success in teaching* (recognized by the PT&E Committee), that should have given me tenure. I believed that then, and I firmly believe it now.

I submitted the documents showing that my second research article has been highly recommended for publication, asking to include them with my tenure dossier, and I also requested a meeting with the Vice-President for Academic Affairs of NDSU, Dr. Allan Fischer. Dr. Fischer was the Dean of the College of Science and Mathematics, but during the 1990-1991 academic year he served as the Interim Vice-President for Academic Affairs.

That was about 45 minutes long (in my estimation) meeting, in his office of the Vice-President. I explained to him that my second submitted from NDSU research article has been highly recommended for publication, and that there were no doubts that it will be accepted for publication. I also brought to that meeting two trunks (two pieces of luggage), each of them of the size about 64 cm x 37 cm x 19 cm (25.2" x 14.6" x 7.5"), full of my research files. I opened these trunks, to show him the amount of my research files - in them.

David, you did all this at NDSU? he asked. "Yes," I answered. (I had more research files accumulated during the years of my work at NDSU, but those two trunks were what I brought to the meeting with him.) He was visibly surprised. And he told me that he would initiate reconsideration of my tenure case.

Reconsideration of My Tenure Starts, but Quickly Stalls

And he did, but the reconsideration quickly stalled. Dr. Allan Ashworth, normally the Assistant Dean, was then serving as the Acting Dean of the College of Science and Mathematics, and he introduced - for my tenure consideration - requirements which were not in accordance with the written rules of such considerations. At the same time, the matter was simple: I had new, important evidence on my research, and I was asking the PT&E Committee to reconsider their recommendation on my tenure on the basis of that new evidence. But the PT&E Committee did not reconsider.

The situation created by all this was extremely difficult for me, and at a certain moment I thought that I was having a heart attack. Somebody brought me to the emergency room of a hospital; fortunately, that was not a heart attack but the result of stress. After that case, I came to the Chair of the Mathematics Department and told him that I could not struggle anymore, because if I continued to struggle, I could end up with a heart attack. And I asked him to represent me in my tenure consideration ("to act in my behalf"), and he agreed.

My Second Submitted from NDSU Research Article Is Accepted for Publication. I Am Denied Tenure at NDSU

In May of 1991, I received a letter with the information that my second (submitted from NDSU) research article had been accepted for publication. I immediately submitted that document to the office of the Vice-President for Academic Affairs of NDSU (Dr. Allan Fischer's office). There were two women working in that office, to one of them I handed the document, asking her to give it to Dr. Fischer.

At approximately that time, the Chair of the Mathematics Department of NDSU told me that he thought that "somebody on the top" of the University did not want me to obtain tenure at NDSU. Later, I received letter stating that my tenure was denied.

If I were in the same situation now as I was at the time of my tenure consideration, I would solve the problem very differently. I would not try to struggle myself, but I would find a lawyer, and I would ask him to handle the situation.

Everything requires experience, but neither my life in the USSR (1937-1977) nor the first period of my life in the USA

(1977-1990) prepared me that it was practically mandatory for me to take legal advice at the first indications of difficulties in the process of my tenure consideration.

My job at NDSU ended in May of 1992. I looked for a job, and I was conducting research as an independent scholar.

Some Things in Life Can Be Understood but Not Proved

And now I shall write about something which is impossible for me to prove, but of the reality of which I am completely convinced. In January of 1993, I came to the conclusion that some of the people whom I considered to be my friends here in Fargo, North Dakota, are people connected to what used to be called the KGB and to the Intelligence Service of Poland.

I was mortally concerned about that. If it was not my friendship, what these people were interested in could only be my research. And if an organization like the KGB were interested to get hold of my research results, then I could lose everything that I accumulated by years of hard work and dedication. And I decided that in the situation in which (I believed then, and I believe now) I was, I needed to start submitting my research results for publication - without delay. I was afraid that otherwise I would lose my research results completely.

In the course of time, I came to the conclusion that some more - than I originally thought - people around me were of the same variety: connected to the intelligence services of the former communist countries Russia and Poland. Again, such things are impossible for me to prove, but this is what I think, this is my firm opinion.

Three of My Research Articles - Submitted After My Job at NDSU Ended - Are Published. I Talk With Dean Allan Fischer

In 1994, three of my research articles submitted for publication from Fargo, North Dakota, after my job at NDSU ended, were published.

In the end of 1994 (I believe), I talked with Dr. Allan Fischer. When I showed him my second submitted from NDSU research article in its printed form, he took notice of the dedication to the memory of my father (printed in the first page of the article) and told that he had never seen that article before.

Well, the original manuscript of that article did not contain the dedication to the memory of my father. Also, at the suggestion of the Editor of the journal, the article was printed with a different (from what was in the original manuscript) title.

Otherwise, Dr. Fischer definitely knew of that article: its manuscript was among the documents submitted by me, in 1990, for my tenure consideration. And in February of 1991, I came to Dr. Fischer and informed him that that article, my second submitted from NDSU research article, has been highly recommended for publication, and I did submit the corresponding documents too.

And in May of 1991, I submitted to the office of the Vice-President for Academic Affairs of NDSU (Dr. Fischer's office at that time) the document proving that that article, my second research article submitted from NDSU, had been accepted for publication.

I have to say that what happened to that document which I submitted - I do not know. When I looked through the files of my tenure consideration several years later, I could not find that document, there were no traces of it.

I Try To Return to NDSU; Four More of My Research Articles Are Published

I wanted to return to NDSU. I believed that I had earned my tenure and was denied it - unfairly. I expressed all this in writing, described my progress in publishing my articles, and submitted that document (addressed to the President of NDSU and to Dr. Fischer). The answer was: "No." Then, in the summer of 1995, I talked with the Vice-President for Academic Affairs of NDSU Dr. Craig Schnell. He told me that he would talk with the Mathematics Department and would get back to me on that matter.

In 1995, two more research articles submitted by me from Fargo, ND, after my job at NDSU ended, were published. I was hoping that Dr. Schnell would get back to me with the result of his contact with the Mathematics Department, as he told he would. The year 1995 ended, and that did not happen. Then I decided to talk with the State Board of Higher Education of North Dakota.

There was a meeting of the Board in Fargo in January of 1996, and that is when I talked with them. I told the Board that I had earned my tenure at NDSU but had not been given it. I also told them that when publishing my research articles, it looked like I had to struggle with organized crime. (I believed in that then, and I am even more convinced of that now.) My appeal to the Board of Higher Education of North Dakota never resulted in any changes to the better in my situation, however.

In 1997, two more research articles submitted by me from Fargo, ND, were published. So between 1991 (when my first research article submitted from NDSU, Fargo, ND, was published) and 1997, I published nine research articles total. Two of them were submitted from NDSU, and seven more - from Fargo, ND, after my job at NDSU ended. These nine research articles were published in seven different journals. Six of these journals were mathematical or applied-mathematical journals, one - an engineering journal.

After 1997 - Not One of My Research Articles Was Published

The two articles published in 1997, however, were the last research articles which I was allowed to publish. I continued doing my research and continued submitting articles for publication, but since sometime in 1996, after I complained to the State Board of Higher Education of North Dakota, each and every new research article submitted by me for publication - has been rejected!

For example, in 2005-2007, I tried to publish a group of research articles. These articles were all interconnected. I first submitted four articles to one journal and one more article - to a different journal. When the four articles in question were rejected in the first journal, I submitted them to the second one. I later added one more article to that group of articles. All these six research articles were rejected, not published!

As recently as in 2014-2015, I tried to publish two new research articles. No way! They both were rejected, each - by three journals in which I submitted them.

As I described above, between 1991 and 1997, I

published nine research articles. And then, in January of 1996, I am talking with the State Board of Higher Education of North Dakota and complaining to the Board. And after that, for about twenty years not one of my new research articles has been accepted for publication!

It is impossible to believe that such a thing can happen accidentally! I think that the organized criminals took note of what I was telling to the State Board of Higher Education of North Dakota in January of 1996 and decided to completely strangle me as a scientist. They decided not to allow me to publish my research results! If I do not publish research articles, I tnen stop existing as a living scientist. As a scientist, I am dead then.

I Discover New Things About My Tenure Consideration - Several Years After the Events

Returning now to the time of my tenure consideration, I have to say that at that time (the 1990-1991 academic year) I did not know that the files of my tenure consideration were accessible to me. I learned that they were accessible to me only several years later, in 1997, and when I learned that, I came and looked at those files.

And then I discovered some new for me things. Very disturbing things.

One of the things which I discovered was the letter from Dr. Allan Ashworth, the Acting Dean of the College of Science and Mathematics, to the President of NDSU, dated 1 February 1991, on the matter of tenure or promotion of a group of professors of the College. A portion of that letter was on the matter of my tenure. That document was never given to me, neither at the time of my tenure consideration nor later.

Reading what Dr. Ashworth was writing in that letter with respect to my teaching at NDSU and with respect to evaluation of my teaching by the PT&E Committee of the College of Science and Mathematics, I could not believe my eyes: I clearly saw that Dr. Ashworth was distorting the truth!

From that letter of Dr. Ashworth, it followed that the Promotion, Tenure, and Evaluation Committee (PT&E Committee) of the College of Science and Mathematics of NDSU could not make a judgement on my effectiveness as a teacher.

And - that was an outrageous distortion of the truth!

The PT&E Committee gave me the letter in which it was written exactly the following: "In the teaching area, we recognize that you have achieved notable success."

Teaching was 60% of my duties at NDSU. When the acting Dean Dr. Ashworth distorts the truth about 60% of my duties, how was I supposed to get tenure at NDSU which I earned by hard work and by dedication to this University and to its students?

Another vitally important thing which I discovered (at the same time, several years after the events of my tenure consideration) was that the document proving that my second submitted from NDSU research article had been accepted for publication - *was not on file!*

Research was 30% of my duties at NDSU, and as I explained above, it was necessary to have *two* research articles submitted from NDSU and accepted for publication to get tenure. Thus, that document, proving that my second submitted from NDSU research article had been accepted for publicatioin, was *vitally, crucially important* for obtaining tenure!

If the document proving that my second submitted from NDSU research article had been accepted for publication - *is not on file,* how was I supposed to get tenure at NDSU?

I shall now give the details about my teaching at NDSU.

Documents About My Teaching at NDSU

First, I shall describe the documents about my teaching at NDSU which were in my tenure dossier at the time when Dr. Ashworth was writing his letter in question to the President of NDSU:

(1) The document *Summary of Student Evaluations,* for the five years of my teaching at NDSU preceeding my tenure consideration, which I submitted for that consideration. In that document, *the quantitative information about my effectiveness as a teacher* was given.

In particular, it was written in that document that in the classes of 25 students or less (senior and graduate courses), the percentage of students who evaluated the quality of my teaching as *Excellent* was 62%, as *Good* - 38%, and as *Average* - 0%. It was also written in that document that in the classes of 26-50 students (freshman and sophomore courses, from the courses for physical sciences and engineering), the percentage of students who evaluated the quality of my teaching as *Excellent* was 59%, as *Good* - 37.5%, and as *Average* - 3.5%. And in the classes of 150-180 students (freshman courses: calculus for the social life sciences and plane trigonometry), the percentage of students who *Liked* my teaching was 81%, who *Liked and Did Not Like* it (at the same time!) was 4.5%, and the percentage of students who *Did Not Like* my teaching was 14.5%.

All these *quantitative data* about my teaching were repeated in the document *Summary Resume* (for the period September 1985 - October 1990), also submitted by me for my tenure consideration.

(2) My *1988 Outstanding Teacher Award*, from the Division of Mathematical Sciences of NDSU, submitted by me.

(3) The document *Comments on Dr. David Tselnik's Teaching of Mathematics Made by Some of His NDSU Students,* five pages, also submitted by me. This document contained comments or excerpts from comments cited by student evaluations, and the purpose of this document was to show which qualities students liked in my teaching.

Also, in my *Curriculum Vitae (*Reporting Period: September 1, 1985 - October 5, 1990), submitted for tenure consideration, I gave the summary of the features of my teaching which, according to the student evaluations, students liked most:

(i)   The ability to explain even very complicated subject matter in a clear, precise, easy to understand manner.

(ii)   That I prepare and use in class my own lecture notes. (My notes were giving thorough and, at the same time, clear and easy to follow account of the material.)

(iii)   That I create a good deal of student-teacher interaction (which helps students to fully understand the subject), and that I have the genuine concern for students.

(4) *Letter of Support for the Case of Dr. David Tselnik, Associate Professor of Mathematics, for Awarding of Tenure at NDSU,* from the Chair of the Mathematics Department of NDSU, with the recommendation to grant me tenure, submitted by the Chair of my Department.

That is what was written in that letter about my teaching at NDSU:

"... David's first experience in teaching mathematics in English language was at NDSU. David has high teaching/ pedagogical abilities. In addition to that, he meticulously prepares an extensive set of lecture notes for each course he teaches (which took most of his time during the first few years here, at NDSU). David's system works very well, as his student evaluations are always overwhelmingly positive, and this is true whether he is teaching pre-calculus, a graduate course, or some intermediate level course. His students often comment on the clarity, precision, and thoroughness of his presentation. He is a popular instructor in Math 130, which is calculus for business and life sciences majors. This is particularly remarkable since this course is seldom liked by the students, when taught by other instructors. In 1988, David was awarded the Mathematical Sciences Division Outstanding Teacher Award, the last year that award was given, attesting to David's reputation as an outstanding teacher ... In summary, I would like to say that David is an excellent teacher."

(5) *Letter,* on the matter of my tenure, from the PT&E Committee of the College of Science and Mathematics, in which letter this is what was written about my teaching at NDSU:

"Your nomination for tenure has been considered by the

College of Science and Mathematics Promotion, Tenure, and Evaluation Committee. ... In the teaching area, we recognize that you have achieved notable success. We particularly recognize and appreciate the dedication and effort that you expend in organizing course materials and interacting with students."

Acting Dean Dr. Allan Ashworth, Describing My Teaching at NDSU, Distorted the Truth

And having all these documents at his disposal, that is what Dr. Allan Ashworth wrote about my teaching at NDSU in his letter in question to the President of NDSU:

"He did not provide any quantitative information by which the Committee could judge his effectiveness as a teacher. He provided some anecdotal information which suggests that his teaching is adequate. He did win a departmental award for teaching."

I shall now "decipher" what Dr. Ashworth maintains in these three sentences, and I shall give my comments.

First of all, Dr. Ashworth maintains that I did not provide any quantitative information about my teaching at NDSU (by which the Committee - he means the PT&E Committee - could judge my effectiveness as a teacher). Here *Dr. Ashworth distorts the truth!* Of course, I provided such information, and I provided it in a very clear and very well organized form - see item (1) above!

Secondly, from what Dr. Ashworth writes, it follows that the PT&E Committee of the College of Science and Mathematics of NDSU could not make judgement on my effectiveness as a teacher. Here *Dr. Ashworth distorts the truth again!* Not only the PT&E Commitee did make a judgement on my teaching, but it judged my teaching at NDSU as *notable success* - see item (5) above! *Notable succcess* - what can be higher than that?

Also, Dr. Ashworth writes that I provided some anecdotal information which suggests that my teaching is adequate, and that I did win a departmental award for teaching.

The meaning of the word "anecdote" in the English language is, I think, somewhat different from its meaning in the Russian language (which is my native). Because of that, it is not easy for me to determine what exactly Dr. Ashworth means when he writes that I provided "some anecdotal information." I think that he refers here to the documents described above in item (3).

However, there were other documents about my teaching at NDSU in my tenure dossier, information in which documents definitely could not be described as "anecdotal." There was my *1988 Outstanding Teacher Award* (see item (2) above) from *the Division of Mathematical Sciences of NDSU* (not departmental, as Dr. Asworth writes), and there was also *Letter of Support...* from the Chair of the Mathematics Department of NDSU (see item (4)), where my teaching was described as *outstanding,* and *excellent*!

But Dr. Ashworth describes, in his letter to the President of NDSU, my teaching simply as *adequate*, and he does not name the Award which I won - by its actual name, *Outstanding Teacher Award!*

Well, if Dr. Ashworth were naming the Award by its actual name, *Outstanding Teacher Award,* he then would not be able to characterize my teaching at NDSU simply as adequate in his letter in question: the words *adequate* and *outstanding* have very different meanings in the English language!

So in the three sentences about my teaching at NDSU, in his letter to the President of NDSU, *the Acting Dean Dr. Allan Ashworth distorted the truth - repeatedly!*

And this document, this letter by Dr. Allan Ashworth, *was never given to me!*

Additional Documents About My Teaching at NDSU Were Included With My Tenure Dossier

The letter in question was written by Dr. Ashworth on 1 February 1991. In February - March of 1991, five new documents about my teaching at NDSU were included with my tenure dossier, some of them submitted by me, and some - written and submitted by others:

(6) I submitted the xerox-copy of the *Christmas Card* given to me by one of my NDSU students. It was written on the reverse of the card in particular the following: "Thank you for your gift of teaching and your concern that I learn." The card was signed, on the reverse, by the first and the last name of that student.

(7) I submitted some additions to *Comments on Dr. David Tselnik's Teaching of Mathematics Made by Some of His NDSU Students (*see item (3) above).

(8) Chairman of the Industrial Engineering & Management Department of NDSU submitted *Letter*, in which letter he wrote in particular the following:

"... the College of Engineering and Architecture and my

Industrial Engineering Department are very dependent on the teaching qualities of the Mathematics Department. Students are prone to tell us who the bad teachers are but not necessarily the good ones. Therefore, I consider it significant that on more than one occasion students have commented that they consider Dr. David Tselnik a good teacher. ..."

I would like to tell here how it happened that the Chairman of the Industrial Engineering Department of NDSU submitted a letter about my teaching. Somebody invited me to come to a church in Fargo on some occasion; what the occasion was, I do not remember. In that church, I met that man, the Chairman of the Industrial Engineering Department. We talked, and he told me that his students were saying that there are only two excellent professors at the Mathematics Department of NDSU: Dr. Robert Vinograd and Dr. David Tselnik. I told him that I was being considered for tenure and asked him to write a letter about my teaching. He did write a letter. He did not write exactly what he told me in that conversation, but as the reader can see, he did write something good about my teaching.

(9) The previous Chair of the Mathematics Department of NDSU submitted *Letter* in support of my teaching activity at NDSU. That is what was written in the final part of that letter:

"... David Tselnik has through hard work, cultivation of natural ability, and dedication contributed considerably to the teaching component of the Mathematics Department's program at NDSU. He has shown over the years that he is an excellent teacher."

I would like to also cite the following portion of that letter:

"David has willingly taken on teaching assignments in trigonometry and Mathematics 130 - calculus for business and the social and life sciences majors. He has shown dedication to these difficult assignments and has been able to develop motivation in a large number of students - not an easy task since most do not enter the class with interest in the technical details required for success in calculus."

(10) One of my graduate students submitted *Letter*, in which it was written in particular the following about my teaching:

"I have studied with many professors of mathematics and the physical sciences during the course of my formal education in physics and mathematics, and I feel that Dr. Tselnik is one of the finest. ... His preparation and presentations are careful and thorough. He displays mastery of his field, while retaining an ability to address the needs of the student. His concern for his students is obvious and genuine, and he is willing to take whatever extra steps are necessary to ensure that they grasp the material in question."

(This student writes about mathematics, and he writes about the physical sciences. Earlier, before NDSU, this student studied on the East Coast of the USA, and he had the Bachelor's degree in Physics from the Massachussets Institute of Technology (MIT). At NDSU, he studied mathematics; after NDSU he studied at the Northwestern University, received Ph.D. degree, and became professor of mathematics himself.)

All these five additional documents about my teaching, (6)-(10), appeared in my tenure dossier during February - the first half of March of 1991.

The Acting Dean Dr. Allan Ashworth had plenty of time to write to the President of NDSU *the truth* about my teaching at NDSU. He never did that! Never!

Interim Vice-President for Academic Affairs of NDSU Dr. Allan Fischer Could (and Should) Interfere, but He Did Nothing

Now, as far as I understand the procedure of tenure considerations at NDSU, from a College, the necessary documents of tenure considerations are passed to the Office of the Vice-President for Academic Affairs (Dr. Allan Fischer's Office at that time), and after that, they are passed to the Office of the President of the University.

When Dr. Allan Fischer, then the Vice-President for Academic Affairs of NDSU, received the documents of my tenure consideration, it was his obligation, his duty - not to allow Dr. Allan Ashworth's distortions of the truth to reach the desk of the President of NDSU!

But Dr. Allan Fischer did nothing.

I Discover New Things About My Tenure Consideration - Several Years After the Events (Continued)

As I mentioned above, there was another very important thing which I discovered after I learned (several years after the events of my tenure consideration) that the files of my tenure consideration were accessible to me.

I discovered that the document proving that my second submitted from NDSU research article had been accepted for publication, that document which I submitted to the Office of the Vice-President for Academic Affairs of NDSU in May of 1991 - *was not on file!*

That document was *vitally, crucially important* for awarding me tenure! That document was the clear proof that I did have two research articles submitted from NDSU and accepted for publication! And thus, that I did satisfy the requirement on the number of research articles necessary for awarding me tenure at NDSU!

Together with that document, I also submitted forwarding letter asking the Vice-President for Academic Affairs of NDSU, Dr. Allan Fischer, to include that document with my tenure dossier. When I was looking through my tenure dossier in 1997, there were no traces of that document and no traces of that forwarding letter - in my tenure dossier! And in other files where I looked - there were no traces of that document or of that forwarding letter. What happened to that document and to that forwarding letter after I submitted them - I do not know.

....

Nothing in my previous (before NDSU) experience prepared me for that in return for the very honest, hard, and productive work, I would get a raw deal at the time of my tenure consideration at a University, in my new country United States of America!

On the Matter of Tenure

Based on my bitter experience of tenure consideration at NDSU, I would suggest making some changes to the rules and procedures of such considerations.

As far as I know, the only person who can grant or deny

tenure at a University is the President of that University. The PT&E Committee and the Dean of the College can only recommend granting or denying tenure, but they cannot grant or deny tenure.

I would introduce the requirement that President of a University, before denying tenure to a professor, must meet with that professor and talk with him, face-to-face. This would eliminate any possibility of misunderstanding or of distortion of the truth by anybody about the performance of that professor. If such procedure existed at the time of my tenure consideration at NDSU, I am sure I would not lose my tenure.

I would also introduce the rule that for each document submitted by a professor for his tenure consideration, a xerox-copy of that document, with the stamp of the proper division (the stamp of College, for example), the date when the document was submitted, and the name and the signature of the person who received it, would be given to the professor. This, I think, would help to ensure that documents would be on file.

There is one more thing which, I think, would be helpful. Many of the professors at American Universities are people who were not born or raised in the United States. These are people who came from different countries where the rules and the customs may be very different from the rules and the customs in the USA. I would hand to each professor a leaflet explaining that the files of his tenure consideration are accessible to him at any time, and also explaining that in the case that he believes that something is wrong in his tenure consideration, it may be proper for him to seek legal advice, to hire a lawer.

Looking Back

I think that from the time when my mother and I moved to Fargo, ND (1985), my life was under unwelcome observation by the Intelligence Services of the USSR (later - of Russia) and of Poland. And for a number of years, until 1993, I did not suspect that.

Such a thing, about observation, is impossible for me to prove. But that is what I think, that is my opinion.

A Guy Tells That I Have Problems With People From Lebanon

Well, as I mentioned above, since sometime in 1996 (after I talked with the State Board of Higher Education of North Dakota), each and every new research article submitted by me for publication has been rejected. And one more thing happened after I talked with the State Board of Higher Education, in 1996. Since then, very often I felt unwelcome attention of organized criminals (I think, I believe) in my everyday life.

Here is one example; it is retained in my memory probably because of the sheer absurdity of what was done (told). I am on the public transportation bus in Fargo, and somewhere near me sits a young man, a foreign student at a University here. I had met that student some time before, at a local store, and I know that he is from Lebanon.

Suddenly, that young man says that he knows that I have problems with people from Lebanon (or he says something very close to that). Not with him personally, he adds. At that moment, the bus stops, and he gets off the bus. I never saw that young man again after that.

Well, who are those people from Lebanon with whom, according to that student, I have problems? I do not think that I had ever met anybody from Lebanon before I came to Fargo, North Dakota. During my life in Fargo, I have met three persons from Lebanon. One was my student at NDSU, and he later married a young woman, from Lebanon too, and later, when I was already not working at NDSU, they invited me, one or two times, to their apartment, to try Lebanese food. So we were friendly, and there were definitely no problems between us. And the third person from Lebanon whom I have met during my life in Fargo was that student on the bus, and he tells that with him - I do not have problems.

So who are those people from Lebanon with whom, according to that student on the bus, I do have problems? The answer is: they do not exist in nature, they are mythical! However, the buses in Fargo are equipped with video and audio recording cameras, and maybe (?) someone has a recording of this incident, where that student tells that I have problems with people from Lebanon!

I do not even know what to call an incident like that: Provocation? Falsification? Both? What I really do not understand is why people agree to participate in such kind of activity? The only possible explanation which I have is that the organized criminals maybe threaten people somehow, to force them to participate in their provocations.

I believe that since 1996, after I talked with the State Board of Higher Education of North Dakota, there were some other attempts to portray me as somebody who has "problems" with this or that group of people.

In particular, I believe that there were attempts to portray me as someone who dislikes people with skin of black colour. These attempts continued for a very long period of time, then stopped. These attempts were not so clearly defined as in the case of "problems-with-people-from-Lebanon" attempt, so I am not describing them here.

One-Semester Job: Teaching Mathematics at the Valley City State University

In 1997, there was an open position in the Department of Mathematics of the Valley City State University (VCSU), in Valley City, North Dakota, and I applied. (That was one of many applications for a position which I sent.) The position which they had was temporary, a one-year position, but they expected to have a permanent position from the next year, and they had the intention to start looking for a permanent faculty. So there was a hope for me to get this one-year position first and then maybe to get a permanent job - at that University.

Valley City is a pleasant small city (population 6585 in 2010), sixty miles to the west from Fargo. The city has hills (as opposed to Fargo, where the landscape is flat), and the river, the Sheyenne River, with a number of bridges over it. I was invited for the interview visit, during which I had to teach a class of students, one academic hour, in College Algebra, to meet with the Search Committee, etc. There were other candidates for that one-year position, who were invited for the interview visits too.

I was later told that the students were asked to vote, and that they voted that I should be hired by the University. The Search Committee, I was told, also voted that the job would be offered to me. But - the job was not offered to me!

I was Citizen of the United States, but the job, as far as I know, was offered to somebody who was neither a Citizen nor a Permanent Resident of the United States, and who, at that moment, did not even have any legal rights to work in the United States! To obtain the permit for that person to work in the United States required time, and the beginning of the 1997/1998 academic year was approaching, but he still did not have the permit to work in the USA.

And then they offered the job to me. Not for the entire academic year but for one semester (the fall semester of 1997) only, with a view that that person will obtain the permit and will start working from the beginning of 1998 calendar year. Not having any job, I accepted the offer. I later asked the Vice-President for Academic Affairs of the Valley City State University, "Why was the job (the entire one-year job) not offered to me?" His answer was, "I don't know."

So during the fall semester of 1997 year, I worked at VCSU. I taught two different courses, one in College Algebra, and one in Calculus, to three diffferent groups of students. I taught fourteen hours per week and came to Valley City, from Fargo, five days per week (as far as I remember). This was about hundred and twenty miles of driving every day. I was able to arrive on time all the days of the semester, with the exception of two. On one occasion, the roads were covered by ice, and I could not move with a speed higher than fifteen miles per hour. So I turned back and called that I would not be able to come. On another occasion, I was about fifteen (or twenty maybe) minutes late for the first class of the day, because of the roads condition. In December of 1997, my job at VCSU ended.

One-Semester Part-Time Job: Teaching Statics at the Department of Mechanical Engineering of NDSU

At the end of 2000, I met a man who was Professor in the Department of Mechanical Engineering and Applied Mechanics of NDSU. It turned out that he was not going to teach in the spring semester of 2001, and the Department needed somebody to teach his load. The Chair of the Department offered me to teach one course, in Statics, to two groups of students during that spring semester. I agreed.

Statics is one of the group of three courses, Statics, Kinematics, and Dynamics, which are the necessary components of engineering education for a number of engineering professions. In the Soviet Union, in every Engineering Institution of Higher Education there was a department named the Department of Theoretical Mechanics, faculty of which department were teaching these three courses; the courses were taught as purely theoretical disciplines, without any elements of engineering in them.

The course in Statics which I had to teach at NDSU had some elements of engineering in it, but not many. I was preparing and teaching a very strong, solid course in Statics. However, there was not much of mathematical contents in that course (so the course goes), and I felt that I was missing teaching mathematics.

In the course of that teaching, I realized that my students could do a lot better if they had better preparation in certain specific questions of mathematics necessary for the course which I was teaching. Those were questions of mathematics not from one mathematics course (subject) but specific questions from different courses (subjects).

I came to the conclusion that it would be a very useful thing to determine *all* such specific mathematics questions, vitally important for teaching of not only Statics but of a variety of courses which NDSU teaches in, say, the first two years of the undergraduate education, and where students could benefit from the better mathematics preparation. And then to create a special mathematics course, one course, the sole goal of which would be to train the undergraduate students in these specific mathematics questions, all of them together (no matter to which different mathematics subjects they belong). This, I am sure, would allow the undergraduate students to succeed in their engineering studies and in other areas of studies much better.

I spoke, in brief, of this simple idea with the Dean of the College of Engineering and Architecture of NDSU, and then I put all this on paper and submitted that document to the Office of the Dean. I never received any response from the Dean's Office. Later, I submitted that document to the Office of the Vice-President for Academic Affairs of NDSU, Dr. Craig Schnell's Office, with the same result: I never received any response from Dr. Schnell's Office too.

No, I Am Not a Mechanical Engineer

My temporary, part-time job in the Department of Mechanical Engineering of NDSU ended in May of 2001. One undesirable consequence of that job was that I started hearing in the places where I was going: mechanical engineer, mechanical engineer, are you a mechanical engineer?, mechanical engineer, mechanical engineer, ... The implication was, I think: you are the Mechanical Engineer, and your place is in a Department of Mechanical Engineering, not in a Department of Mathematics.

Well, I am not a Mechanical Engineer and never was.

Part of my education, immediately after the high school, was in Naval Architecture (Shipbuilding), and due to that part of education, I am a Naval Architect. I did teach some courses in two Departments of Mechanical Engineering in the USA: at Stevens Institute of Technology (I mentioned that job above) and at NDSU. The courses which I taught at these Departments - Mechanics of Materials (Strength of Materials), Statics, and Fluid Dynamics Laboratories - are common to many engineering professions, they are not specifically mechanical engineering courses.

No, I Am Not an Architect

That spell, "mechanical engineer," continued for several years. After those years, I was "transformed" into Architect! All I heard then was: architect, architect, architect, ... Again, with the implication, I think: you are the Architect, and your place is in a Department of Architecture, not in a Department of Mathematics.

In a store, in Fargo, I talked with a woman (I live alone, and I talk with strangers wherever I go; there is nobody to talk with in my apartment). That woman told me that her husband is a faculty member in the Department of Architecture of NDSU. Next time I saw that woman, in a different store, she was with her husband, and he invited me to come to the Department of Architecture.

Department of Architecture? What was I supposed to do in the Department of Architecture? Architecture, as far as I understand, to a very large degree is Art, and I have no abilities to Art, whatsoever! I can try to draw a horse, for example, and everybody will see, I am sure, that the animal in my drawing has four legs and one tail. However, that will not be an enjoyable picture of a horse.

Naval Architecture, which I studied immediately after the high school, is Science; one does not need to have abilities to Art to be able to study Naval Architecture.

That "architect" spell was short-lived, and it died a long time ago.

About Hearing Loss, Macular Degeneration, and Diabetes

After I was denied tenure, I applied for jobs in the Department of Mathematics of NDSU for many years, and somebody - or somebodies - in this City of Fargo (criminals, I think) were trying to find out whether I have, or to demonstrate maybe that I do have some kind of impairment which would preclude me from performing my duties as a professor.

The first subject of their attempts was, I believe, my hearing. If somebody is placed close to me, and if I talk with that person, and if that person speaks unusually quietly, or unusually fast, or with a heavy accent, then I may ask that person to repeat what he just told. That is normal, but at the same time, somebody who is acting not in good faith - may try to use this as a demonstration of my bad hearing. I think that that trick was used many times. Well, there is nothing wrong with my hearing, and I never had any problems to maintain a normal conversation.

The second subject of their attempts was, I believe, my vision. Suddenly, I heard "macular degeneration." I did not even know what that was. I had to look and to find out that that is a disease of retina, eye disease. Well, I do use glasses when I read, and I am required to use glasses to drive, but that is all. Otherwise, there is nothing wrong with my vision.

For some period of time, there were attempts, I believe, to attribute diabetes to me. People whom I did not know tried to find out whether or not I am buying sugar, or they were trying to suggest sugar-free products to me. Well, I do not buy sugar, but I like sweet things - honey, for example, or chocolate. These attempts - about diabetes - continued for a considerable period of time, then stopped.

I described not all the attempts of this kind here, but let us stop and go to something more meaningful, to my research interests during the Fargo period of my life.

My Research Interests - During the Years of Work at NDSU and in the Later Years

As I have already mentioned above, I started doing research at NDSU sometime in the spring of 1986. By that time, my research intertests deviated from what I was doing (mostly) before that. My research became less applied-mathematical, and more, or mostly, pure-mathematical.

I was researching representations and series expansions for meromorphic functions. For the reader who is not a mathematician, and who does not know what meromorphic functions are, I shall mention that such trigonometric functions as tangent or cotangent - are the examples of meromorphic functions.

I was researching series expansions of Jacobian elliptic functions. Elliptic functions are, in some respect, more general than trigonometric functions: trigonometric functions are periodic functions, they have period, and elliptic functions are doubly-periodic functions, that is, they have two periods.

I was researching series expansions of the functions called theta$_{1-4}$ functions and of their logarithmic derivatives. Theta$_{1-4}$ functions are closely connected to elliptic functions. And I was researching solutions of integral equations.

The elliptic functions, the theta$_{1-4}$ functions and their logarithmic derivatives, and some of the integral equations are used in solving problems of physics, mechanics, and engineering.

I have to say that the basis for my new research was in my previous work in the field of the Theory of Jets, in my previous experience in applications of the Theory of Functions of a Complex Variable (which theory I started to study at the age of eighteen on the advice of Professor Maksim Isidorovich Gurevich).

What Is Applied Mathematics?

One thing I have to clarify here. I just wrote that my research became more, or mostly, pure-mathematical. Pure-mathematical, or applied-mathematical, it depends on the definition of what applied mathematics is. There is no distinct boundary between pure mathamatics and applied mathematics. Moreover, some mathematicians do not believe that applied mathematics exists.

For example, J.H. Poincare (1854-1912), a famous French mathematician (and engineer), did not believe that applied mathematics exists. Of the same opinion was V.I. Arnold (1937-2010), a well-known mathematician born and educated in the Soviet Union. As far as I understand, these mathematicians were of the opinion that there is mathematics and there are applications of mathematics, not such a thing as applied mathematics (on this matter, see http://en.wikipedia.org/wiki/Applied_mathematics).

I shall give here two quotations, from what I found on the web, on the subject of what applied mathematics is, representing different opinions.

"There are different views of what applied mathematics is. For example, a purely mathematical study of a differential equation arising in an applied problem can be, and is considered by some, to be applied mathematics. Our view is different. Applied mathematics, as we view it, is the application of mathematics to real-world problems ... ." (This quotation is from Engineering Sciences and Applied Mathematics, McCormick School of Engineering, Northwestern University, http://www.esam.northwestern.edu/about/what-is-applied-math.html.)

"Applied mathematics is the development and the application of mathematical methods for solving real-world problems and problems derived from science and technology." (This one is from School of Mathematical Sciences, Tel Aviv University, http://www.math.tau.ac.il.)

These two quotations represent two points of view on what Applied Mathematics is.

According to the point of view of the McCormick School of Engineering of the Northwestern University, Applied Mathematics is the application of mathematics (to real-world problems).

According to the point of view of the School of Mathematical Sciences of the Tel-Aviv University, Applied

Mathematics also includes the development of mathematical methods for solving real-world problems.

My research during the years of work at NDSU, and later in Fargo, ND, was almost exclusively in the area of mathematical methods, mostly those methods which can be used in applications. However, almost exclusively - it was not in the area of applications of mathematics to concrete applied problems.

If one accepts the point of view of the McCormick School of Engineering of the Northwestern University, then my research during the Fargo period of my life should be qualified as being, almost exclusively, pure-mathematical research.

On the other side, if one accepts the point of view of the School of Mathematical Sciences of Tel Aviv University, then my research during the Fargo period of my life should be considered to be predominantly applied-mathematical research (and only partially - pure-mathematical research).

My opinion is that an Applied Mathematician is a person who applies serious mathematics to solving problems of the real world. At the same time, I think that a person who is researching mathematical methods - however useful they are, or can become, in applications - without actually using those methods for solving real-world problems, should be looked upon as a Pure Mathematician, not an Applied Mathematician.

Somebody who is a Pure Mathematician and somebody who is an Applied Mathematician may judge the value of a mathematical result from different points of view. A Pure Mathematician may judge a specific mathematical result the more valuable the more difficult it was to obtain that result, the more complicated its derivation was. An Applied Mathematician may judge a specific mathematical result the more valuable the more useful that result is in applications, in solving real-world problems, irrespective of what was the level of difficulty to obtain that result.

I Wrote and Published a Mathematics Research Book

Let me now return to the matter of publishing of my research results. Seeing that, starting from a certain moment in 1996, after I complained to the State Board of Higher Education of North Dakota, and for many years after that, each and every research article which I was submitting for publication was rejected (not accepted for publication), I finally decided that the way for me to publish my research results would be to write a book based on the results and to publish that book.

To set forth the main material of the book, I needed to have six chapters in the book, and the book is primarily on the subject of series expansions. So I named the book "Six Chapters on Series Expansions." I wrote that book and published it, myself, in 2012 Ref. [5].

The main mathematics subjects in my book in question are Compex Variables (subject number 30 in 2010 Mathematics Subject Classification of the American Mathematical Society and of Zentralblatt Math of Germany) and Special Functions (subject number 33).

The book is based partially on the results previously published by me in journals, but predominantly - on the results not previously published, a number of which results I was not able to publish (not allowed to publish) since 1993, or from 1996 and up to 2007.

Remark. *Description of the* Mathematics Subject Classification *can be found on the Internet.*

As a Mathematician, I Am an Applied Mathematician

More accurately, as a mathematician, I consider myself to be *mostly* an Applied Mathematician, but also, *partially*, a Pure Mathematician.

My book Ref. [5] can be considered to be, I think, partially an applied-mathematical book and partially a pure-mathematical book. To what degree it should be considered an applied-mathematical book, and to what degree it should be considered a pure-mathematical book, depends on one's definition of what applied mathematics is.

My Second Mathematics Research Book

In 2013, I self-published one more mathematics research book. This book is entitled "The Function Xi_*" Ref. [6], and it contains my research results of different years, some of them obtained many years ago, and some obtained much closer to the time when the book was published. Mathematics in this book belongs to the subject Special Functions - subject number 33 in 2010 Mathematics Subject Classification, and the book is a pure-mathematical book (mostly).

Again, Looking Back

Looking back at my life in Fargo, I believe that if at the time of my tenure consideration I had gone to a lawyer, instead of trying to struggle myself, I would not have lost my tenure at NDSU.

However, I am not sure that I would have been able to survive in my University position for a long period of time. If those are the Intelligent Services of the former Communist Countries, the Russian Intelligence, the Polish Intelligence (as I think), who organized systematic rejections of my research articles in journals, they could have done this irrespective of whether I had a position at University or not. And if my research articles were not being published for a considerable period of time, I would then be out of the University, period.

That denial of tenure at NDSU - extremely unfair, I believe - turned my life in the USA upside down. I survived - because I was deeply engrossed in my research.

Since sometime in the 1990s, for many years I have been applying for jobs in the Department of Mathematics of the North Dakota State University. They never gave me any job! Never! So after many years, I stopped applying for the positions they advertised.

As a Scientist

Looking back at my life, I believe that as a scientist I have done the maximum I could.

I published twenty seven research articles (between 1965 and 1997), in a variety of journals - in mathematical journals, in applied-mathematical journals, in journals on applied mechanics, in engineering journals - and in other editions.

(In Appendix Two, the list of journals and other editions in which the research articles written by me were published is given.)

Not one of my research articles was published after 1997, but that is not because I did not try to publish them. I think that the systematic rejection of all my new research articles submitted for publication after sometime in 1996 (after I talked with the State Board of Higher Education of North Dakota) was organized, and I think that those are the Russian and the Polish Intelligences who organized it. To prove that I cannot, of course, but that is what I think, that is my opinion.

I wrote and published myself, in 2012, mathematics research book "Six Chapters on Series Expansions" (mentioned above), ISBN 978-0-9837324-3-3; 401 pages.

I also wrote and I published myself, in 2013, another mathematics research book, "The Function Xi_*" (also mentioned above), ISBN 978-0-9837324-0-2; 114 pages.

My published articles and my two mathematics research books contain most of the research results which I obtained in the course of my scientific activity (but not all).

I did not describe in this book any of the research results which I obtained during my life in science. The research results are for the scientists in the corresponding fields of science to evaluate, and this book is written for the general reader, not for scientists only.

Part Two

OTHER RECOLLECTIONS

Chapter 3

More About The Events In My Life

This chapter contains a collection of stories with the description of various events in my life, mostly of the time when I lived in the USSR but not only of that time.

When I Was Two-and-a-Half, and When I Was Five

When our family, my father, my mother, and I, lived in Kamenets-Podolsk, my parents had friends in the city, a couple whom they knew, I think, from their Odessa time. The couple had a daughter, of approximately my age.

One day my parents and I were visiting that family. The adults were talking, and at a certain moment they realized that their children - that daughter and I - were missing. Worried, they started looking for us. They found us walking along a bridge across the river. (There was the river named the Smotrych River in Kamenets-Podolsk, and there were bridges over that river.)

It turned out that I decided to show that girl the place where my parents and I lived, and so I started walking with her towards that place.

I myself have no memory of that case, I was not older than two-and-a-half when that happened. What I am telling you now - my parents told me.

When I was five, and my mother and I lived in the city of Sverdlovsk (today - Ekaterinburg; located on the Ural Mountains), I was in the kindergarten. Not far from the building where that kindergarten was, there was a cemetery, and there were bushes with raspberries at that cemetery. Sometimes our teacher (mistress) took us, a group of kindergarten children, to that cemetery, and we were happy to eat raspberries.

One day I invited a girl from our group of children to go to that cemetery, just the two of us, to eat raspberries. That story is in my memory because I was then old enough to remember what happened. I only do not remember what was the punishment - if any - when our teacher discovered that we were missing ...

Well, I think these two cases show that I was a pretty independent fellow even when I was very young. I think, that quality stayed with me all my life, for better or for worse.

Story of the Stolen Flounder

That happened in 1942 (or in the beginning of 1943 maybe), also when my mother and I lived in evacuation in Sverdlovsk. We lived on the first floor of a big apartment building in somebody else's apartment, and we had one room in that apartment.

As I mentioned before in this book, food was always a problem in the evacuation. When we had normal food to eat, we were glad, of course. But sometimes we were eating unusual dishes, such as, for example, the stinging nettle soup (where there were only two components: stinging nettle and water), or potato peels, somehow (but I do not remember how) prepared.

One day my mother was able to buy a flounder, the whole

fish of flounder! Mother probably had the intention to cook the fish the next day, so it was necessary to keep the fish fresh - somehow. I am saying somehow because there was no refrigerator in the apartment where we lived. (In the USSR, at that time, probably very few people had refrigerators in their apartments. At least, I did not see a refrigerator in anybody's apartment until many-many years later.)

Fortunately, that was in a cold time of the year, and Mother placed the flounder between two frames of the window. (Windows in the USSR had two frames, the outer frame and the inner frame, and each frame could be opened independently.) And we went to sleep.

In the morning, we discovered that our flounder was gone. Somebody cut off a portion of the glass of the outer frame and stole our flounder!

Story of the Piano Which I Never Got

That happened in 1945.

As I mentioned above in this book, the Army to which my father's artillery unit belonged finished the war (the Second World War) at the German city of Konigsberg. The Soviet Union was going to annex that city, so the Soviet authorities told the German population of Konigsberg, in 1945, to move out and to go to mainland Germany.

The Germans had possessions, of course, but they did not have the transportation to move them to mainland Germany. So they needed to sell many of their possessions.

At the same time, the officers and the soldiers of the Soviet Army were given some German money (German marks), and they could buy things from Germans.

One thing which my father bought with the money he was given was a piano for me. (I was then eight years old and wanted to learn to play piano.) My father's artillery unit had trucks (American Studebaker trucks, I think), and my father could move that piano.

Sometime after the war ended, my father's artillery unit was moved to Belorussia (a USSR's Republic in the European part of the Soviet Union; today - an independent country, the Republic of Belarus) and stationed there in some wooded area.

One day, a superior of my father came to him and told him, "Lieutenant, we know that you bought the piano for your son. But we want to open the officer's club, and we do not have a piano for that club. Would you donate that piano for the officer's club?"

My father had to say "Yes," and that is how I never got that piano. I never even saw a picture of that piano, and the only thing I know of that piano is that it was made from redwood (Father told me that) ...

Some Memories of the Time of the Second World War

Here is my very first memory of the time of the Second World War: two planes in the sky and a column of light from the ground to the sky. That is my memory of the summer of 1941. I was then four-and-a-half years of age, and I do not think I could understand - then - what that meant.

Some time later, when I was old enough to understand, I could interpret what that my memory meant. Those were two planes in the sky above the city of Moscow. One was a German bomber, and another one was a Soviet fighter, and that fighter was trying to shoot that bomber from the sky. And there was a projector light directed to the German bomber, and trying to blind the pilot of the bomber.

After my mother and I returned to Moscow from the evacuation, in October of 1943, I remember there was a park of (captive) balloons somewhere in the area where we lived. Such balloons were kept close to the groung, but at the times of the air attacks, they were raised in the air, to create balloon barrage, to make work of German bombers more difficult. However, at that time, and later, there were no German bombardments of the city of Moscow anymore. So these balloons were probably kept as a precaution.

I remember that after big victories in the war, there were big fire works in the sky of Moscow.

I also remember that in 1944 (I think), there was a big exhibition of the captured German armament in Moscow: tanks, guns, planes. The exhibition was in the Gor'kii (Gorky) Park, on the bank of the Moscow river.

The last memory of that war were some German prisoners of war. I saw a small number of them working in our neighbourhood. They were fixing fences. Well, it is better to do the job of fixing fences than to invade a country, especially the country (the USSR) with which Germany had the agreement of non-agression, and to start a war where millions of people were killed. Some time after the war ended, the German prisoners were sent back to Germany, and I did not see them in our neighbourhood anymore.

Shoes

In the first grade of school (or in the second grade maybe), for a period of time, I had no shoes.

In the years of the Second World War, not only food was rationed in the USSR but also some goods. To buy shoes or clothes, one needed to have coupons. And my mother did not have the coupon to buy me shoes.

So she took a thick fabric, put some kind of wadding between two layers of that fabric, and hand-stitched someting to put on my feet. Above that someting, I was wearing galoshes (rubber galoshes), and that is how I was coming to my school for a period of time, until my mother was able to buy me shoes.

As far as I remember, I was the only pupil in my class who did not have shoes to come to school. However, shoes or no shoes, I was bringing home A's, or almost always A's.

Satchel

What I also did not have, for some period of time in the years of school during the Second World War, was a satchel, to put my textbooks and notebooks into it. We had a canvas bag, of the green color with the red cross on it. Such bags were used in the army by medics, and how that happened that we had that bag, I have no idea. I used that medics' bag - as a satchel.

Another Case of Anti-Semitism

Above in this book, I described how a group of boys

started beating me, in my early shool years, because I was a Jew.

There was another case of the manifestation of anti-semitism in my early school years. A boy was telling something anti-semitic to me, in the presence of other boys, in my school. What exactly that was that he was telling, I do not remember.

I told that to my mother, and she came to talk with the parents of that boy. My father was in the army, fighting at the front. That boy's father was in Moscow, not in the army (he was not drafted).

After my mother's conversation with his parents, that boy never opened his mouth for the anti-semitic utterances.

Some of the boys, pupils in my school, were definitely contaminated by the virus of anti-semitism.

Ice Cream

Sometime in 1944, when I was seven years of age, my grandmother Hana bought me, on a street of Moscow, a pack of ice cream.

And - I did not know what that was. I presume that I enjoyed ice cream, from time to time, before the Second World War. However, I had no memories of that, I was too young then to remember. In the cities where we lived during the evacuation, I never saw ice cream. And after we returned to Moscow, I did not see ice cream until that moment in 1944.

By the way, the sellers of ice cream on the streets of

Moscow were sometimes attracting customers advertising their product as follows,"*Sladkoe kak Med, Kholodnoe kak Led!*" In translation into the English language, that means, "*Sweet as Honey, Cold as Ice!*" (In the Russian language, these two lines are rhymed, and they sound better than in my English translation.)

Commercial Food Stores

During the time of the Second World War, food in the USSR was rationed. To buy any kind of food in stores, a person had to have coupons: coupons for bread, coupons for butter, coupons for milk, etc.

However, sometime in the last (I think) year of the war, the Government opened a chain of other food stores, the chain of the Commercial Food Stores. In such food stores, a person could buy products without coupons, but the prices were higher than in the usual food stores.

I remember one such commercial food store, on the Taganskaya square in Moscow. My mother and I were at that food store a couple of times. Those stores were for the people who had money. My mother definitely did not have money to buy food in such stores regularly, but my father, being an officer in the army, was given money certificates, and he was sending these certificates to my mother. With these certificates, my mother bought some food in that commercial food store.

Buying Bread Without Coupons

In a certain year after the Second World War (in 1946 maybe?), the rationing of food in the USSR was stopped, and people could then buy food without coupons.

On the first day that bread could be bought without coupons, my father and I came to the bread store in our neighbourhood, before the time the store was going to be opened. There was a crowd of people, who also came to buy bread, in front of the store. And there was a militsioner (policeman), whose duty was to make sure that buying bread on that special day would go smoothly.

At a certain moment, the militsioner gave the command, "Form the line from this point," and he extended his hand. The people were rushing to get a place in the line, and the line was formed. The store opened, and people were buying bread without coupons, as much bread as they wanted to buy. After many years of bread (and other food) rationing, that was a happy experience!

Abundance of Food

In the first years after the Second World War, food was still a problem for us (for my father, my mother, and me). In the beginning of the 1950s, that changed. Food was abundant in the Moscow food stores in those years.

The city of Moscow was supplied by food better than other cities in the USSR. That is because there were the Foreign Embassies in Moscow, and the Soviet Government wanted to show the foreigners who worked in those embassies how good is the life in the USSR.

Some of that food was very tasty. Not far from the place where we lived, there was a small food store. In those years (in the beginning of the 1950s), that food store always had the red caviar of three grades and the black caviar of two kinds. The red caviar was the keta caviar (keta is a variety of the fish salmon). The keta caviar of the lowest grade was of approximately the same price (per weight) as butter, and the price of the keta caviar of the highest grade was about two times higher.

Years later, caviar almost disappeared from food stores.

Greek Olives

During the Second World War, I never saw olives in food stores, and I did not even know that such a product exists. After the war ended, at some moment, olives appeared in food stores. Those were the Greek olives (marinated olives), and they were sold by weight, not in jars. Their name in the Russian language was - Masliny.

My mother and father, being grown up in Odessa, where some people were ethnically the Greeks, and where the Greek olives was a popular food, were very familiar with that food and they loved it. So one day (in 1946 or in 1947 maybe) they bought these olives in a store. I tried one olive, and I spitted it out: the taste was very unusual, and I did not like that taste. "Well," my parents told me, "we are asking you to try to eat the olives for one week. If after that you still do not like them, we shall not try to persuade you."

I tried for one week, and after that I considered the Greek olives to be one of the most tasty foods. Later, when I was married and had a daughter, my daughter, being a child, was used to eat the Greek olives.

One day, my daughter got ill, and her doctor told us, her mother and me, that in order to recover, our daughter needs to eat the black caviar. The black caviar, which was in every Moscow food store in the beginning of the 1950s, practically disappeared from the stores by the time my daughter was born.

One of our acquaintances was able to buy a small ,100 grams maybe (about 3.5 ounces), can of the black caviar for us, and I was glad to offer it to my daughter. Daughter, however, told me, "I do not like it, and I will not eat it!" Well, she did not even try the black caviar; it was the case of the childish obstinacy.

Then I told my daughter, "Don't you see? These are simply the Greek olives for children, that is what they are!" Indeed, caviar is the fish eggs, and each egg of the black caviar resembles a Greek Olive, only it is much-much smaller in size than a Greek olive

"Oh," told my daughter, "these are the Greek olives for children? I love them!" And she ate the caviar, and she recovered.

When we - my mother and I - lived in Rome, Italy (on the way to the United States, for about two weeks), there was a small Farmers Market near the place where we lived. People were selling, among other food products, homemade (marinated at home) Greek olives at that market. These were the best Greek olives I ever tried!

Going to the Bathhouse

In the aparment where we lived in Moscow before and, for more than a dozen years, after the Second World War, in the school building, there was a bath-tub. Probably we used that bath-tub in the pre-war times. However, after we - my mother and I - returned to Moscow from the evacuation, we could not use that bath-tub anymore. Somebody used it to hold liquid ink (which pupils and teachers of the school needed for writing) during the time that we were in the evacuation. Whatever we did after that, the water in that bath-tub was always of some "inkish" color and not proper for bathing.

   My father and I were going to a bathhouse, usually one time per week. That bathhouse was located at a distance of about 50 minutes (or so) of walking from the place where we lived. And, for some period of time, there was no city transportation from the place where we lived to that bathhouse. So we had to walk (at that time).

   That bathhouse had bathing rooms for men, bathing rooms for women, a swimming pool, a barber shop, and a place where one could buy and drink kvass or beer.

   Kvass is a Russian non-alcoholic beverage. When Napoleon's army invaded Russia, the French soldiers called kvass - "pig lemonade" (or something close to that they called kvass). For the Russian palate, kvass is tasty. In summers, there were always on the streets of Moscow cisterns with cool kvass. One could buy and drink a mug of kvass and then continue his walk.

   The bathing rooms in that bathhouse were of two categories, a cheaper one and a more expensive one. How they were different, I do not remember. We normally used the cheaper one. In the bathing rooms, there were the cement benches, faucets with cold and hot water, showers, and sauna (or something like sauna, with steam and with the birch besoms.)

   The cement benches were flat, and one could seat or lie on such a bench. When lying on the stomach, another person could wash your back.

   A person could, for an additional charge, have somebody to wash him, to wash his back, for example. We - my father and I - did not need that. There were two of us, and we could wash (and massage a little) each other's backs. The birch besoms in sauna were to lightly lash yourself (or somebody else, if he asked for that).

After the bathing, we - my father and I - were usualy drinking kvass and resting, maybe 30 minutes or so. After that, we were walking home, another 50 minutes.

That bathing - in the bathhouse - was a considerably more substantial experience than using the bath-tub at home.

Short-Wave Radio-Receivers

Until 1947, we - my father, my mother, and I - had in our apartment one-station radio. We could turn that radio on, or turn it off, or make it louder, or make it quieter, but that was one and the same radio station all the time. That radio station, I think, was called the Moscow City Radio-Network.

In 1947, my parents bought the short-wave radio-receiver. For the reader who is not familiar with what the short-wave radio-receiver is, I shall mention that that is the kind of radio which allows to listen to distant radio-stations. The receiver which my parents bought was called Vostok (in English: East), Model 7H27 (in English: 7N27). It was one of the first short-wave radio-receivers produced in the USSR soon after the Second World War.

That receiver had seven tubes. And it had the short-wave bands and the medium-wave band (in the USA, that band is called AM). I do not remember what shortwave bands that receiver had. I am not sure it had the 11 meter band or the 13 meter band. Probably it had the 15 or the 16 meter band and all the broadcast short-wave bands with the wavelengths longer than that.

   Although that receiver was made in the USSR, however, much later, when one of the tubes of the receiver failed and had to be replaced, I discovered that all the tubes of the receiver were made in the USA. As many short-wave receivers of that time, that receiver had the "green eye," a tube producing wonderful green light, glowing on the front side of the radio. The purpose of that green eye was to show how well the receiver is tuned into a radio-station.

   That receiver brought a number of the radio-stations of the USSR broadcasting in the Russian language, and it also brought many stations from abroad broadcasting in many different languages to our home. I do not remember whether the radio-stations broadcasting in the Russian language from abroad, such as the Voice of America, or the BBC, or Deutsche Welle, were being jammed by the Soviets in 1947, but probably they were. Nevertheless, sometimes it was possible to hear some small portions of such broadcasts.

   And there was an abundance of good music, jazz in particular, on the shortwaves during those years.

   We never had a good antenna for that receiver (or for any of the short-wave receivers I had in the USSR after that one), just a piece of wire in the room where that radio was. However, the propagation of the radio-waves in Europe is much better than, for example, in the American Midwest where I now live, and that primitive antenna was sufficient to hear many stations.

   Eventually, that receiver went out of order. My second short-wave receiver was a trophy Philips-Telefunken, which somebody brought to the USSR from Germany, or maybe from Austria, after the Second World War. My father-in-law had that receiver, and he did not use it and gave it to me.

That Philips-Telefunken had only four tubes, but somebody explained to me that those were somewhat unusual tubes, each of them replacing two ordinary tubes.

That radio, as a shortwave receiver, was not as good as the first one, Vostok, but it was outstanding as a medium-wave (AM) receiver. Sometimes I was able to listen, in Moscow, to good music from Italy using that receiver on AM. That receiver, however, was difficult to repair, and there were no tubes for that receiver in the USSR. Eventually that receiver went out of order, and it had to be abandoned.

My third - and the last - shortwave receiver in the USSR was the big and expensive radio called Festival' (Festival). That was a very good looking radio, with a good sound. It had three speakers, two of the round shape on the sides of the radio, and one of the elliptical shape on the front. In addition to the short-wave and the medium-wave (AM) bands, that receiver also had the ultra-short-wave band (called FM in the USA).

For the medium-wave (AM) band, there was a magnetic antenna inside that radio, and that antenna could be rotated using a knob on the front panel of the radio - a wonderful convenience for the medium-wave (AM) listening!

As far as I remember, at the time when I had that radio, Festival', the Soviets were no longer jamming broadcasts in the Russian language by such stations as the Voice of America, the BBC, or Deutsche Welle. Only it was a good idea not to make the sound too loud, that your neighbours would not know that you are listening to those stations.

In the years when I had these three short-wave radio-receivers in the USSR, they were a good source of good music and, at certain times, of the news from abroad.

When I Was Eleven

When I was eleven, my parents told me that they wanted to talk with me. They told me that the system of the Soviet Union was a bad, rotten system, that what was written in the newspapers was not necessarily true, etc. They told me that there were severe repressions in the USSR, especially in 1937, the year I was born. They told me that in that year they had to destroy their correspondence with some other people, which they had. (Maybe those people were arrested, or maybe they were foreigners, and my parents were afraid that if the Government finds that correspondence, they could be repressed too.)

They told me that they decided to talk with me because they wanted me to live with open eyes and not to be deceived by the Soviet propaganda. They told me not to talk about what they told me with my classmates.

Since I was twelve, or thirteen maybe, I started to believe in the United States. I started to believe that there should be a country with a good system, and that such a country is the United States of America.

When I Was Thirteen

When I was thirteen, on my birthday my parents gave me a present, a watch. That was a mechanical watch of those days; it had to be wound every day in order to continue to work.

Today, everybody has a watch. At that time, in my class, only one or two boys had watches. I was so impressed, I could not sleep all night after that. I was looking at my watch!

When I Was Fourteen

When I was about fourteen, I wrote this small verse:

Zhizn' grustna. Byvaet pravda veselo,
No obychno ochen' grustno byvaet.
Zhizn' kak dereva odinokogo vetka,
Veter rvet ee, treplet, kachaet.

And here is my translation of this small verse into the English language:

Life is sad. Occasionally, it can be merry,
But usually it is very sad.
Life is like a branch of a lone tree.
The wind tries to rend the branch from the tree,
It flutters and shakes the branch.

Well, I was fourteen when I wrote these lines. Now, when I am writing this section of the book, I am eighty one. Was my life sad? Was it lonely?

I shall share my thoughts about that with the reader - later in the book.

Fountain-Pens

When I was in school, the writing was done with the liquid

ink (of the violet color, as far as I remember). We used wooden penholders with metal pens. Pens of different designs could be bought and inserted in those penholders. Such a pen, naturally, had to be dipped into the ink-well, and rather often. We, boys of our class, wanted to do something that pens could hold a bigger volume of ink. So we were making small spirals (using thin metal wire), and we were fixing those spirals on the inside of the metal pens. Those were our primitive "fountain-pens."

After the Second World War, the officers and the soldiers of the Soviet Army brought home fountain-pens made in Germany, in Austria maybe, etc. I had one such fountain-pen. It was made from some light metal alloy, had a piston system of filling, and also had two transparent slot windows - so that the level of ink inside the pen could easily be observed.

I always liked fountain-pens. In the Soviet Union, I used a number of them, mostly made in the USSR. The best fountain-pen which I had in the Soviet Union, however, was made in China. As far as I heard, the Parker company had a fountain-pen factory in China. After China became what was called the communist country, that factory became probably the property of the Chinese Goverment. And - that factory continued making some model (or some models maybe) of the Parker fountain-pens.

Once, a shipment of those fountain-pens was sent to Moscow, the USSR. The pens were with a golden nib, but some bureaucrat in Moscow did not realize that, and he set a very low price for those fountain-pens. I bought one and enjoyed writing with it - until one day somebody borrowed that pen, and I never saw it again.

(Earlier in life, I had a similar experience. When I was in

my first year of engineering education, after the high school, I bought a cheap guitar. That was the Russian guitar, with seven strings, and I learned - a little - how to play it. Then one day somebody borrowed my guitar, and I never saw it again. And I completely forgot how to play the guitar.)

When we - my mother and I - came to America, I had a fountain-pen with golden nib made in the USSR. That pen was a gift from my grandmother Hana. Somehow, I lost it.

So I needed a new fountain pen. In an office supply store where I came to buy a new fountain pen, there were pens made by Sheaffer, Montblanc, probably Parker. I had a rather small amount of money in my pocket, and with that money I bought a fountain-pen made by Sheaffer. That pen was called "Targa." I still have that pen. I worked with it for probably four or five years. But - I always wanted to buy a different fountain-pen, with a golden nib maybe.

Since the Fall of 1979, for several years, we - my mother and I - lived not far from the New York city, 50 or 60 minutes by bus from New York. One day, when my mother and I were in New York, we were walking along some street, to the north of the main building of the New York Public Library, and in the window of some shop, there were a number of fountain-pens displayed. My mother looked at those pens, pointed at one of them, and told me, "This pen would be good for you." Later, I learned that that was the Montblanc Model 146 (which is called Le Grand).

Several times we - my mother and I - were in New York in the store called, as far as I remember, Art Brown and Company. That was an office supply store, and it had a big section with fountain-pens and with drawing instruments, too. Mrs. Brown, who was one of the owners of that store, was selling fountain pens, and she told me that the best fountain-pen is Montblanc. She herself had and used the biggest in size Montblanc fountain-pen, called Diplomat.

The Diplomat was too big for my hand. The Le Grand (model 146) was of a good for me size. One day, we - my mother and I - were in Washington, D.C., and not far from the White House, we came across a pen store, Fahrney's Pens. We came inside, and I told the salesman that I am interested in the Montblanc 146, with the fine nib. He told me that they just received from Germany seven Montblancs 146 with the fine nibs. He put all of them on the counter, gave me a sheet of paper and a bottle with the Montblanc ink. I could dip the ends of the nibs of those pens into that bottle, and I could write using those fountain-pens (on the paper).

It took me one-and-a-half hours to choose one pen from those seven. My mother was patiently waiting for me. That is how I bought my Montblanc Model 146. I did a lot of research work using that pen.

I had and used a couple of other good fountain-pens in the USA. However, the Montblanc 146 was the best fountain-pen I had in my life.

And - it was my mother who told me originally that that pen would be good for me!

How did she know?

Foreign-Made Cars

Since the time I was a boy, I was interested in cars. In the foreign-made (made outside the USSR) cars, in particular.

The foreign-made cars were rare in the USSR. In that respect, Moscow was in a somewhat different situation. There were many Foreign Embassies in Moscow, and those Embassies were using, I believe, the foreign-made cars. If their countries were producing cars, those Embassies were using, I think, the cars made in their respective countries.

For example, I remember that once, when I came to a concert of Classical Music in the Big Hall of the Moscow Conservatory, the car with the British Ambassodor drove up to the entrance of the Big Hall. That was a Rolls-Royce. The American Embassy, I think, was using the American-made cars, etc.

Some number of the foreign-made cars could always be seen on the streets of Moscow. In particular, after the Second World War, some German Opel-Kadetts, Opel-Olympias, Opel-Kapitans, and Opel-Admirals were brought to the USSR, and those cars could sometimes be seen on the streets. Those cars were not new.

For a period of time after the Second World War, the Soviet Union was receiving reparations from Germany. As a part of those reparations, a number of the new BMW cars were received from Germany, and they could be seen on the streets of Moscow too. Also, the new German cars called DKW.

I saw on the streets of Moscow other foreign-made cars, too. For example, Packard, Volvo, Volkswagen,Tatra (made in Czechoslovakia).

When a foreign-made car was parked on a street of Moscow, the car usually attracted the attention of the passers-by.

When we - my mother and I - lived in Italy, on the way to the United States, there were many cars on the streets of Rome, mostly of a rather small size. Probably Italian-made or made in other European countries.

When we came to the United States, in 1977, the cars on the streets and the roads were large, much bigger than the cars in Italy.

My first car in the United States was Chevrolet Monte Carlo. When we came to Fargo, in 1985, I was looking for a new car. There was a dealership in Fargo selling the Swedish SAABs at that time. When seated at the steering wheel of a new dark blue SAAB, my mother told me, "You look good in SAAB."

Well, I did not buy that new SAAB. I bought a big, used Oldsmobille 98, very comfortable for my mother.

My current car is the Mercury Sable. For a number of years, it has been sitting in the garage. It needs repair, and I am not sure what to do with that car ...

One more thing I want to add here. About the foreign-made motorcycles. For a period of time immediately after the Second World War, the Moscow Militsia (Police) were using the American Harley-Davidson motorcycles.

Pastry Shop Elnem

In the center (downtown) of Moscow, on what was called the Stoleshnikov Lane, there was a pastry shop which everybody called the Pastry Shop Einem.

The pastry enterprise Einem was founded in Moscow by the immigrants from Germany in the 19th Century. In the Soviet times, that shop definitely had some official name different from Einem, but people continued to call that shop by its pre-revolution (the revolution of 1917) name: Einem.

That shop made some of the best (if not the best) pastries in Moscow. When our family was expecting visitors, my mother always asked me, or my father, or both of us, to go to that shop and to buy pastries for the visitors. We lived very far from the center of Moscow, and it was possible, of course, to buy pastries at a local food store. But the Einem pastries being of the best quality, it was worth that to spend time, and to go, and to buy the Einem pastries.

The shop was selling eclairs, napoleons, and many other kinds of pastries. One kind was called "the potato." There was no potato in that pastry, but it was in the shape of potato and of the color of the unpeeled potato. These pastries were sold by piece. There were also the same kinds of pastries but of a small "child" size. These were sold by weight. All kinds of pastries that shop was selling - I simply do not remember.

I do not know how long the Einem shop was located on the Stoleshnikov Lane. I do know, however, that when my Professor at Aspirantura, Maksim Isidorovich Gurevich, was a boy, his father sometimes took him to that shop to enjoy pastries. At that time, the shop probably had some space with tables, and people could eat pastries and to drink tea, or coffee, or cocoa (hot chocolate) - at the shop. In the years when I lived in Moscow, there were no tables in the shop, and people could only buy pastries - to take them home.

The Einem company had, in the pre-revolution times, a

big factory in Moscow, making chocolate and candies. That factory continued to work in the Soviet times too, only its name was changed, some time after the revolution (of 1917), to The Red October.

In the summer of 2018, I was in a Fargo store that sold Balkan and European food. I bought something, and was also given a small candy. "This is a Russian candy," the cashier told me. The candy was wrapped, and on the wrapping it was written, "Iris, Zolotoi Kliuchik, Krasnyi Oktiabr'." In translation into the English language, that means, "Toffee, Golden Key, The Red October."

I definitely consumed some amount of that candy when I lived in the USSR. That small candy told me that The Red October factory in Moscow still exists, and that although Russia is not a communist country now, the name of the factory is still The Red October.

Eliseevskii Store

The Pastry Shop Einem was not the only store which people continued to call by its pre-revolution name, even sixty years after that revolution. In the center (downtown) of Moscow, on what was called in the Soviet times the Gor'kii (Gorky) Street, there was a Gastronomical Store (Grocery and Provison Shop, Food Store), which everybody called the Eliseevskii Store.

Eliseev was the last name of the man who owned that store before the revolution (before1917). And that store definitely had some official name, different from Eliseevskii, in the Soviet times. However, even sixty years after that revolution, people continued to call that store by the name of its pre-revolution owner!

That store was in an old building, and beautiful inside. I do not think that I ever bought any food at that store, with the exception of two things: *pirozhki s miasom and vatrushki s tvorogom.*

The first one was made from a dough with ground meat inside. The second one was also made from a dough but with curds (of the sweet taste) on the top. Both were tasty and not big in size, and when I was in the center of Moscow, walking along the Gor'kii Street and hungry, it was convenient to buy one or both those things and to eat them while I continued walking.

Studying the English Language

I was in the sixth grade of school when I started to study the English language. As every pupil in school, I had to study a foreign language, one foreign language. However, to choose what foreign language to study - I could not. We had two classes in the sixth grade of our school, class 6A and class 6B. The administration of the school decided that class 6A would study English and class 6B would study German. I was in class 6A. So I studied English. Those studies continued until I graduated from school. We had a very good teacher of the English language, and I liked English.

After the high school, at Mosrybvtuz, where I studied Naval Architecture, I studied the English language for, I think, four semesters (two academic years). During each of those semesters we, students studying engineering, were required to translate a certain amount of pages of the English technical texts into Russian. Usually, students translated adapted (simplified) technical texts. That was, of course, easier than to make translations of texts not adapted.

I had no desire to use any adapted texts for translation. The Library of Mosrybvtuz had American and British journals in the field of shipbuilding, and I was translating articles from those journals. In the beginning, that was unbelievably difficult. Later, I could translate those articles with ease.

At Aspirantura, I had to study English too, but for only a short period of time (for one semester, I think).

By the time we, my mother and I, came to the USA, I had considerable experience in reading English mathematical and technical texts. However, the experience of conversation in the English language, I did not have. A sentence of somebody's speech often sounded to me as one big strange word. And when I bought for the first time a bowl of soup and wanted to know how much I should pay for it, instead of asking "How much?", I asked "How many?" I knew that I should ask "How much," but ...

I listened to the radio, watched TV (looking at the lips of people when they were talking), tried to talk with people as much as I could, and tried to talk with people over the telephone. The latter was most difficult - because I could not see the lips of people when they were talking. The first time I had to talk over the telephone with somebody about some scientific conference in the English language, my shirt became wet on my back!

My efforts paid off. I gained sufficient experience in conversational English. Much later, when I was invited to teach at NDSU, and we came to Fargo, my mother told me, "If you want your students to understand you, speak slowly." And that was a good advice. I remember one student wrote in his evaluation of me, "Nice accent. Makes me listen."

At certain times in my life, I tried to learn two other foreign (for me) languages, French and German. Both times that was because I wanted to read some mathematics books which were available - one in the French language only and another one - in the German language only. Both times I did study the grammar of the corresponding languages, but that was all. I never had time to learn French or German.

Until a certain year, people who wanted to become Kandidat Nauk (Ph.D.) were required to know two foreign languages. Later, knowledge of only one foreign language was required.

By the way, Professor M.I. Gurevich, of whom I already wrote in this book, knew four foreign languages: English, French, German, and - to a certain extent - Italian.

Helping My Mother in Her Work

For a number of years before I was in the last (10th) grade of school, my mother worked as an insurance agent.

As every enterprise in the USSR, insurance was governmental. There was one organization, called Gosstrakh, whose activity was insurance. Gosstrakh means Gosudarstvennoe Strakhovanie. In translalion into the English language, the State Insurance.

In our district of Moscow, there was a local office of Gosstrakh. There was the Head of the office, and there were a number of insurance agents. To each insurance agent, a certain area of the district was alloted.

So my mother had an area of the district alloted to her. Mother had to come to the office from time to time only. Her main task was to find people in her area of the district who "could be persuaded" to buy an insurance policy (an accident insurance policy, for example), to persuade them to buy it, to insure them, to collect (usually one time per month) the insurance premiums from them, and to deposit, at the end of each working day, the collected money into a savings institution.

My mother was very good at that job. She was friendly, and she could explain to people the advantages of being insured very well. She was able to insure a considerable number of new customers. Mother was respected by the customers and at the office. The advantage of this job for my mother was that her working schedule was very flexible. Also, my father and I could help her in that job, and we did that.

Sometimes my mother would tell me to go to a certain customer, on a certain day, and to collect his insurance premium. I would go, collect the premium, and give the customer the receipt prepared by my mother in advance. Or, at the end of a working day, my mother would give me the money collected during that day (cash; there were no personal checks in the USSR) and would send me to deposit it into a savings institution.

Only my mother and my father knew that I was doing that. The reason was simple: sometimes I had a considerable amount of money in my pocket, and if that were known, I could be robbed.

French Buns, City Buns, and Related Matters

In the Moscow bread stores, there were buns called the French buns. They were very tasty (to my taste), and I was buying them rather often. Until one day, when I came to the bread store in our neighbourhood and discovered that there were no French buns in the store anymore.

That is, there were the buns in the store looking exactly the same as the French buns. And they were of the same taste. But they were not called the French buns anymore. They were now called the City buns. Overnight, the Government renamed those buns!

I think, that happened sometime in the 1950s. That was in the period of time when the Soviet Government was emphasizing the priority of the Russian scientists and inventors over the priority of the scientists and inventors foreign. The name French buns was the victim of the same campaign.

Tarzan Movies and Other American Movies Which I Saw in the USSR

Sometime in the very beginning of the 1950s (I think), in the movie theaters of Moscow three or four American Tarzan movies were shown. Where the Soviets got the films of those movies, I do not know. Maybe they bought them from the company which made those movies, or maybe they captured, during the Second World War, some film depository in Germany, and that is how they got the films of those movies.

We - my mother, father, an I - lived then not far from a big ball-bearing factory. Its name was "The First State Ball-Bearing Factory." That factory had a club named "The House of Culture," and there was a movie theater in the building of that club.

So many people wanted to see those American Tarzan

movies that the administration of the club had to put additional chairs - in the aisles of that movie theater!

The movies which were shown in the movie theaters in the Soviet Union were usually the movies made in the USSR. However, sometimes the foreign-made movies, American, French, etc., were also shown. Those were shown not necessarily with their original titles.

For example, in the USSR, I saw the American movie titled (in translation from the Russian language) "There Are Only Girls In Our Jazz-Band." Only when we - my mother and I - were living in America, I learned that the original title of that movie was "Some Like It Hot."

Well, if that movie had been offered in the USSR with its original title, "Some Like It Hot," translated literally into the Russian language, I do not think that the Soviet audiencies would understand from the title what that movie is about. "There Are Only Girls In Our Jazz-Band" was incomparably more understandable.

Among the American movies which I saw in the USSR, there were (if I remember their titles correctly) "Twelve Angry Men," "Nuremberg Trial," and "Wedding Lunch." The American movies were among the best (if not the best) movies which I saw in the USSR. Spencer Tracy was the actor whose name I knew from those now distant times.

She and I, Combinedly, Saw Two Tyrants: Stalin and Hitler

It was the seventh of November of 1951, and I was then in the ninth, last but one, grade of school. On the seventh (and on the eight) of November of each year, the Soviet

Union celebrated the Communist Revolution of 1917. On the seventh, there was always the military parade in the Red Square in Moscow, and after the parade, there was what was called the demonstration of workers.

On the seventh of November of 1951, all the pupils of my grade, and probably of some other grades of my school, together with our teachers, were required to take part in the Red Square demonstration. All the distance from the school to the Red Square we were required to cover by walking. My school was located very far from the Red Square. We assembled at the school building in the morning and started walking.

Moscow was covered by snow that day. During the walk, we had to stop several times, since people from different factories, institutes, and pupils and teachers from other schools were also walking towards the Red Square, and we had to wait for our turn to go forward.

(My father was also walking towards the Red Square on that day, together with pupils of some grades of the school where he worked and with some other teachers of that school.)

Somebody was coordinating the movements of groups of people, militsia maybe. Finally, in the afternoon, around 3 PM maybe, we approached the Red Square. When walking in the Red Square, we had to walk rather fast.

On the Lenin mausoleum (a building in the Red Square where the body of Lenin is preserved), there was a group of people. Those were the members of the political leadership of the Soviet Union, Stalin among them. That is how I saw Stalin, from a distance.

When I was working at NDSU, there was a woman working then in the NDSU bookstore. She emigrated to the USA after the Second World War from Germany. She told me that when she lived in Germany, she saw Hitler on a parade.

Thus, she and I, combinedly, saw two tyrants of the 20th Century: Joseph Stalin and Adolph Hitler.

By the way, I just mentioned the Lenin mausoleum. Lenin died in 1924, and his body was preserved. I was inside the Lenin mausoleum one time. We, the pupils of my class in school, were required to go to that mausoleum, together with one of our teachers. The visit to that mausoleum brought me into an oppressive mood, and I never visited the mausoleum again.

Ballroom Dancing

In our school building, on the second floor, there was a big hall. That hall was normally used as a gymnasium or for meetings. The hall had a very good wooden floor and was also used as a ball-room.

When I was in the next to last grade of school (in the ninth grade; I was fourteen when I entered that grade), there was a ballroom dancing class in my school. The class was held by evenings, two times per week, for the most part of the academic year. The duration of each lesson was two academic hours in a row.

That class was an after-school activity. I decided to learn the ballroom dancing, and I took that class. A number of other boys, pupils from my boys' school, were also taking that class, and a number of girls, pupils from the girls' school where we, my father, my mother, and I, lived and where my father was the director (principal) before the war, were also taking that class.

   We had an excellent teacher for that class. He was a professional ballet dancer. In the USSR, two opera and ballet theaters had the best in the country ballet companies. One was the Bol'shoi (Big, Large, in translation into English) Theater in Moscow, and another one was the Kirov (formerly, and now - Mariinskii) Theater in Leningrad (St. Petersburg).

   Our teacher of dancing was a member of the Bol'shoi Ballet Company. He was not a star, not a soloist, but a member of the corps de ballet in that company. Teaching us ballroom dancing was an additional, part-time job for him.

   I liked that dancing class, and I was good in the ballroom dancing. Until one day I jumped from one step of a stairway to another step of that stairway in some building, and something cracked in my foot. That was the end of my ballroom dancing lessons then. By that time, the class covered probably seventy five or eighty percent of the program. After that, I could not attend the dancing class. However, from the window of the apartment where we - my father, my mother, and I - lived, I could see the windows of the ball-room in our school, and I could see, from a distance, that lighted hall and the figures of pupils dancing in that hall.

   There was another time in my life when I attended the ballroom dancing class. I was then in my early thirties and worked at the Institute for the Problems of Mechanics of the Academy of Sciences of the USSR. My then doctor told me that, for the benefit of my health, I needed to do some physical activity where my feet would move a lot.

   In the center (downtown) of Moscow, there was The House of the Teacher, teacher's club. My father being a teacher, I knew of that club, and I was in that club several times.

   Once I saw a notice that the club invited people to participate in the ballroom dancing class. I applied and was accepted. That club was located in a building which before the revolution of 1917 was a hotel (I think). It had a ball-room of a modest size, with good wooden floor, and with one wall covered by the mirror.

   The duration of that class was about one academic year. The classes were held by evenings, two times per week, for two academic hours in a row for each lesson. The people taking that class were of different ages. The youngest was a girl, a school pupil, of seventeen years of age, and the oldest was a retired professor of seventy years of age.

   Our teacher of ballroom dancing for that class was a faculty member of the Department of Dance of the Institute of Culture (if I remember the name of that Institute correctly) in Moscow. Sometimes, when he would give us a rest, he would tell us the history of the dance which we were learning.

   This time I did not jump from one step of a stairway to another step, and nothing cracked in my feet, and I was able to attend all the lessons in that class from the beginning to the end.

   Ballroom dancing is, in my opinion, a wonderful healthy activity. Once learned, the ability to ballroom dance can serve a person for the duration of his or her lifetime. At least, for a long period of time - normally.

Photography

When I finished the ninth (the last but one) grade of school, in 1952, my parents bought me, on my request, a camera. That was the 35 mm Zorkii, the first model of that Soviet camera, a copy of some model of the German camera Leica.

That Zorkii was built so fundamentally, that I think if I needed a hammer and did not have one, I would be able to use my Zorkii instead! I bought a book on photography, read it, and started making photographs.

That was the black-and-white photography, on a film, and then one had to develop that film in some solution, in a dark room. After drying, the film was ready to be used for printing photographs. In a dark room again, on a photographic paper, using a printing device. After developing, in a different solution, the photopgraphs had to be dried, and that was the end of the process.

I had all the necessary equipment and was making photographs, including developing film and printing photographs, myself. The photographs were black-and-white, but they could also be made brown.

After I became a student at Mosrybvtuz, I had very little time for photography. I made only a small number of photographs during my student years. I have a photo of my daughter when she was a baby, made by me in the spring of 1959, and that was probably the last photograph which I made myself.

Before leaving the Soviet Union, I sold that camera, Zorkii. I do have two other 35 mm cameras: Zenit (made in the USSR) and Praktica (made in East Germany). In the USA, I was not making photographs myself. And I used my cameras only a few times during the years that I have lived in the USA. The last time I used my cameras was in November of 1987, one month before my mother died. I photographed my mother then.

The modern camera, the digital one, I do not have.

My daughter, who now lives in Israel, likes photography. Maybe she inherited the interest in photography - from me?

Some Vacations

I had a considerable number of vacations during the time that I lived in the USSR, but only some of them left deep traces in my memory. Among those, the vacations which we - Father, Mother, and I - had in 1947, 1950, and 1955 in Moldavia.

During summers, my father, being a school teacher, had a long vacation time. I think, it was eight weeks. In the summer of 1947, our family went on vacation to Rybnitsa, in Moldavia, the place where my father was born and where we had relatives. We took a train, from Moscow to some place in the Ukraine, had to transfer to another train, and that train brought us to Rybnitsa. That was the first time in my life that I was on vacation.

In the years immediately after the Second World War, the officers who served in the Soviet Army during that war had a special perquisite: one time per year they could take a round trip by train to any place in the USSR - for free. In

1947, my father used that perk.

Later, that perk was abolished. In 1950, when our family went on vacation to Rybnitsa the second time, my father had to pay for his train ticket.

Our third vacation in Moldavia, in 1955, was in the village called Rashkov. As Rybnitsa, Rashkov was situated on the left bank of the Dniester River. After vacationing in Rashkov, our family spent several days in Rybnitsa, with our relatives.

I have a photograph of some place in Rybnitsa which I made using my Zorkii camera in 1955. I am looking at that photograph now, and I see a one-story dwelling house built from limestone (there were the limestone hills in the vicinity of Rybnitsa) and the limestone fences - around this house and another house. I also see the trees inside the fences, the unpaved road in front of the houses, and the Dniester river- at a distance.

Our relatives in Rybnitsa lived in the house of the same type as I just described. The trees in their yard were the apricot and the walnut trees. Our relatives, husband and wife, had two daughters. One of them was of my age. Being ten (in 1947), she and I would climb a walnut tree and spend some time sitting on the branches of that tree and talking.

Sometimes the adults and we, the children, would go to the bank of the river and swim. I remember one time there was a horse on the bank of the river, and the horse was wet, and I was wet too (after swimming). I never had a horse so close to me, and I decided to climb that horse. And I did climb the horse, but the next moment I fell down. That was the only time in my life that I was on a horse. For a few seconds maybe, not longer.

There was a Farmers Market in Rybnitsa. On certain days, called bazarnye dni (the bazaar days), a big number of farmers would bring their products to sell at that Farmers Market. One could buy a live chicken at that market, home-made butter (usually wrapped in cabbage leaves), home-made Brynza cheese (a cheese made from sheep's milk), home-made grape wine, and many other agricultural products usually sold at farmers markets.

The Dniester River, at Rybnitsa and at Rashkov, is wide. And there was a boat (ship) going along the river, from town to town. That is how we came from Rashkov to Rybnitsa in 1955, by boat.

The lands on the different banks of the Dniester River had different names. The land on the left bank was called Moldavia, and the land on the right bank was called Bessarabia. Before the revolution of 1917, both these lands were in the Russian Empire. For a period of time after that revolution, Moldavia was in the USSR, and Bessarabia was in Romania, a different country.

Jews who lived in Rybnitsa had relatives on the right bank of the Dniester, in Bessarabia. But when Bessarabia became a part of Romania, they could not cross the river and visit their relatives. My father told me that at that time people were coming to the banks of the river, on two different sides, and communicating with each other shouting as loudly as they could ...

One time, during our Moldavian vacations (in 1947, I think, that happened), my father had to go from Rybnitsa to Kishinev, then the capital of the Moldavian Republic (now - the capital of the country of Moldova), before the end of our vacation. And my mother and I had to come to Kishinev to join him - later. And so we did. Somebody had to carry a Jeep-type vehicle, loaded on a truck, from Rybnitsa to Kishinev. And we, my mother and I, were inside that Jeep.

That turned out to be - initially - not a pleasant experience. The truck was moving along the unpaved road, the Jeep was jerking, and we, my mother and I, were constantly jerked up and down, and often the head of my mother, and maybe my head too, were hitting the roof of the Jeep. Only when my mother put me on her lap, these hittings stopped ...

Coming back to Moscow after the vacations in Moldavia, my parents were bringing home a big (of the size of a large piece of luggage) wicker backet with grapes. My father knew how to pack grapes that they would remain in good shape after the trip from Moldavia to Moscow. They had to be packed tightly.

One time, when my parents brought home grapes from Moldavia, they bought a very big glass bottle and made grape wine from those grapes.

....

In 1953, after I was admitted to Mosrybvtuz, I was, in summer, on vacation in Sochi, a resort on the shore of the Black Sea. I was on that vacation with a family of our relatives, husband, wife, and two sons. One day we went to a forest in the vicinity of Sochi. After a long walk, we were resting under an old tree. And then we got up and started walking again. Suddenly, we heard the cracking noise. The old tree under which we were sitting just a minute or two ago, was falling. If we were still sitting under that three, it could kill or injure us. Fortunately, we got up at the right time.

My another vacation in Sochi was when I was in my thirties. That was in a sanatorium, in the summer time too. That sanatorium was located very close to the beach but above the sea level. Two of us, patients at that sanatorium and complete strangers, had one room - with a big balcony, with the unobstructed sea view. To come to the beach and back to the sanatorium, we used a funicular: two coaches, and when one coach was going up, another coach was going down.

There was a bath treatment for patients at that sanatorium, but all other time we were free to do whatever we wanted. Food was served three times a day, and each day we could order dishes for the next day, from a menu. In the evenings, there were dances at our sanatorium on some days and at other sanatoriums on other days, and we could come to those dances. The duration of that vacation was four weeks, and that was one of the best vacations I had in my life.

When Stalin Died

Stalin died in March of 1953. I was then sixteen and in the last grade of school.

When Stalin died, his body was placed, for a short period of time, at some hall in the center (downtown) of Moscow. The place was open to the public - that people could come and to say good-bye to Stalin. So many people were coming that crushes were created. A number of people were crushed to death in Moscow then.

My parents worried. I was not at home, and they did not

know where I was. They worried that I went, with my schoolmates maybe, to the center of Moscow, to say good-bye to Stalin. I, however, had no intention to go and to say good-bye to Stalin. I was in the Library of the Ball-Bearing Factory (which was the nearest library to the place where we then lived), reading some books. When I came home, my parents breathed with relief: I was alive, not crushed to death.

Sport, Books, and the Moscow Libraries

In sport, I was below average. In front of the building of our school, there was a ground of a sufficient size to use it to play football. When I say football, I mean the European football, which in the USA is called soccer. (I never even heard of American football when I lived in the USSR.) I was not good at football: I could not run fast enough, and I was not good as a goalkeeper too.

I could swim, however. I could play volley-ball. And I liked skiing. When I was in my early thirties, once I was on vacation at a place near Moscow. That was in the wintertime. The place was surrounded by woods, and I was skiing in the woods for a couple of hours each day of that vacation.

Being below average in the sports activity, what I liked - were books. Books and libraries.

The first book that I remember I have read was "Don Quixote," by Miguel de Cervantes. I was then not even seven years old. I read that book, but some other books which we had (from the pre-war time), I put into our stove. (That was after we, my mother and I, returned to Moscow from the evacuation.) That stove could work on fire-wood, coal, or peat, but we had neither of them. To cook food, to be able to eat hot food, we had to use books as fuel. Fortunately, that continued only for a short period of time. My mother bought a kerosene oil-stove, and we did not have to burn books anymore.

In my school years (1943-1953), I was reading a lot of literature. The nearest library to the place where we lived when I was in school was the Library of the Ball-Bearing Factory (as I mentioned above). That was not a particularly big library. It had one reading room of a modest size. I was in that library a number of times.

At a longer distance from the place where we then lived, there was the Palace of Culture of the Moscow Automobile Plant. Still, it was only at a distance of twenty-five or thirty minutes of walking. That Palace was a very impressive cultural center, and it had a very substantial library. I used that library sometimes when I was in school.

The biggest library in Moscow was the Lenin Library. (Today that library is called All-Russian State Library.) That was the biggest library in the USSR (and one of the biggest libraries in the world). I started using that library when I was in high school, and I was in that library many, many times after I received my Diploma of Naval Architect.

Another very big library in Moscow was the Library of the Moscow State University. I was in that library a couple of times when I worked at the Institute for the Problems of Mechanics.

There was also the Library of Foreign Literature in Moscow. (Today, it is called All-Russian State Library of Foreign Literature.) That library I also used, but only sometimes.

And of course, all the Institutions of Higher Education and the Research Institutions - and they were numerous in Moscow - had their own libraries. The city of Moscow was rich in libraries.

Engineering Drawing

As I mentioned above in this book, my teacher of drawing in school told my father that I had the lowest abilities in drawing of all the pupils of my class. Well, studying Naval Architecture (at Mosrybvtuz), I had to master the subject of engineering drawing. We had a very serious course in drawing. It consisted of two parts: the mechanical engineering drawing and the shipbuilding drawing. The duration of that course was three semesters.

The Department of Engineering Drawing of the Bauman Moscow Higher Techical School had the reputation, I believe, of being the best such Department in Moscow. Somebody told me that our Department of Engineering Drawing, at Mosrybvtuz, had the reputation of being the second best.

The drawing was then made in pencil, or in Indian ink, on the drafting paper called the Whatman paper, or in Indian ink on the tracing paper. I spent a lot of time mastering engineering drawing. At the end of the third semester, one of my shipbuilding drawings, of the size of a full sheet of the Whatman paper (I do not remember the measurements of such a sheet, but it was a big-size sheet), was framed and put on the wall in the hallway of the Department of Engineering Drawing of Mosrybvtuz.

The engineering drawing, it turned out, could be mastered. The artistic drawing, however, I do not believe I would be able to master. One needs a special gift from God for that, I think, and that gift - I do not have ...

Studying Higher Mathematics at Mosrybvtuz

The Department of Higher Mathematics of Mosrybvtuz was teaching us engineering mathematics. The courses started from the Calculus and the Analytic Geometry and then progressed to the Differential Equations and to all the other courses in engineering mathematics which we had to study.

For mathematics, we had to be in class ten hours per week. Three times per week, we had lectures, and the duration of each lecture was two academic hours, with a small (five or ten minutes) break between those hours. And two times per week, we had the class where we were solving problems. Again, the duration of each class was two academic hours, with a small break between the hours.

There were two women who taught us mathematics. One of them, Dotsent (Associate Professor), was Kandidat of Sciences (Ph.D.), and she lectured us on mathematics. Another one, Assistent (Assistant Proferssor), had a diploma on the Master's degree level, and she was solving problems with us.

As far as I remember, we studied Higher Mathematics for four semesters. During each semester, we had two, or three maybe, tests. The duration of each test was two academic hours, and during those hours, we were solving problems. The purpose of these tests was both for our professors and for us, students, to check how we were doing. These tests did not count, however, at all towards the final grade for the course. The final grade for the course was given on the basis of the final examination only.

The final examination in mathematics for the first semester of the academic year was in January and for the second semester, it was in June. Before the final examination, we had three or four days for preparation. On those days, we did not have any classes. One time during those days, we could come and ask our professor questions.

The final examination was oral. It usually started at 9:00 AM and continued until 3:00 PM, or 4:00 PM, or later, until all the students of the group (usually about twenty five students or so) were examined. At 9:00 AM, our proferssor would invite five or six students to enter the room where the examination was held. There was a table in that room, and on that table, there were a number of cards with typed or handwritten questions for the examination. Each card contained questions in theory (lemmas, theorems, and their proofs), three questions maybe or so, and problems to be solved, maybe three problems.

The questions and the problems to solve on different cards were different, not the same. The student could not see the questions and the problems; the typings or handwritings were facing the table. The student could only see the number written on the back of the card, nothing else.

The student had to choose one of the cards, only then he was able to read the questions. If a student knew all the material equally well, it did not matter much, of course, what card you picked up for your examination. However, sometimes a student who did not know all the material of the course equally well, could find out that the questions on the card he picked up were not to his liking. He then could ask to pick up a different card. However, his grade for the examination on the basis of that second card would be automatically lowered. If his answers to the questions of the second card deserved A, he would be given only B, not A, for the examination. If his answers to the questions of the second card deserved B, he would be given C for the examination, etc.

The time which a student could use to answer all the questions and to solve all the problems on the card was not limited. When the student was ready, he could raise his hand or tell the professor that he is ready to be examined.

Professor was examining students one after another. During the examination, the student had to deliver a small lecture on the subject of each question and to show the solutions to the problems which he prepared. The professor could ask student additional questions, and so it was a very thorough face-to-face examination.

Each student had an examination book where the professor would write all the information about that examination, the subject, the date, etc., and the grade given for that examination. However, before writing that grade into the examination book, the professor would always tell the student what grade he wanted to give him.

For example, the professor could tell the student, "I believe that you deserve B." The student could agree, and then he would get B. However, if a student believed that he knew the subject better and deserved A, he could ask the professor to ask him more questions. The professor would normally agree to that. In some cases, the student could show, on the basis of the additional questions, that he really deserved A. Then the professor would give him A.

Students who study in the USA would find the number of hours in class per week we had for mathematics, the procedure of the final examination, and how the final grades were given - to be very different from the corresponding numbers or procedures in the USA.

Sailing Practice

As I mentioned above in the book, one of my Practices, when I was a student studying Naval Architecture, was the Sailing Practice, on a ship, at sea. My Sailing Practice was on a crab-fishing ship, at the Sea of Okhotsk, in the summer of 1956.

This is how the Sea of Okhotsk can be found on the map. To the west of Alaska, there is the Bering Sea. To the west of the Bering sea, there is the Kamchatka peninsula. To the west of that peninsula, between the Kamchatka and the mainland Russia, the Sea of Okhotsk is located.

To come to that sea from Moscow, I had to first cross the territory of the Soviet Union, from Moscow to Vladivostok. By train, it took about eleven days and nights. At a certain day, the train was going along the shore of the Baikal Lake, and at a stop, the locals were selling to the passengers of the train the fish called Omul' (Omul). That fish, a delicacy, is specific to the Baikal Lake.

The flotilla of the crab-fishing ships (several of them) was at sea when I came to Vladivostok. To reach the flotilla, I had to first sail on a supply ship from Vladivostok to the place at the Okhotsk Sea where the flotilla was at that time. The flotilla was at sea several months in a row, and the supply ships were necessary to bring the flotilla food and whatever else they needed.

Our supply ship was scheduled to leave the port of Vladivostok on Friday, the 13th. Probably the captain of our ship believed that leaving port on Friday, the 13th, could bring bad luck. So he did everything - not to leave the port on that day. When the clock was several minutes past midnight, and that was already Saturday, the 14th, our ship left the port!

To reach the sea of Okhotsk, the ship was going through the La Perouse Strait, which is between the Sakhalin and the Hokkaido Islands. However, I did not see that strait. It was the night time, and I was sleeping. Later, our ship stopped at the Paramushir Island, an island in the Kuril Islands chain.

The crab-fishing ship to which I was assigned (her name I do not remember) was, in fact, a big floating factory producing canned crab-meat. It was built in Sweden (I believe) and was used originally as a log transporting ship. Sometime after the Second World War (I think), it was bought by the Soviet Government and sent to San Francisco, USA, to be re-equipped, to become the crab-fishing ship.

The actual catching of crab was done using modest-size fishing boats, which people called by some Japanese name. Two names come to my memory: *kawasaki* and *dori*. Which one of these two was the name that people called those fishing boats, I don't remember. (Well, my sailing practice was more than sixty years ago.) The crab-fishing ship had a number of such fishing boats situated on her deck.

Crab is a creature which moves along the bottom of the sea, and the nets were lowered from the fishing boats to the bottom of the sea. Then, after a certain period of time, the nets were lifted, together with caught in crab.

On the deck of the ship, crab was removed from the nets. Crab were big in size and heavy. People removing crab from the nets worked in special gloves - to protect their fingers and hands from the crab claws. If bitten by the crab claws, it was not easy to cure that.

Crab was then put in a metal latticed container, and the container was put in boiling water, and crab was boiled. After that, the container with crab was put outboard, in the sea water, to cool the boiled crab. Crab was then processed, and the canned crab-meat was produced.

Being on that crab-fishing ship, I was at every place of the ship which was possible to reach, and I studied how the ship was constructed very thoroughly.

When the time came for me to go back, another supply ship brought me to Vladivostok. The way from Vladivostok back to Moscow took only eight days and nights. That was a faster train, an express train, that I took on the way back.

By the way, when I arrived at that crab-fishing ship, I discovered that there was a plenty of the red caviar, excellent keta caviar, in the food storage of the ship, but people were not eager to eat the caviar.

Well, it was possible to eat that caviar by table-spoon, and for a few days, I did it. After that, I stopped eating caviar: there was so much salt in the caviar that my body could not tolerate consuming it anymore!

For the supply of the fresh food, people depended on the supply ships. On one occasion, when the supply ship was not coming for a longer than usual period of time, there were no fresh eggs in the food storage of our crab-fishing ship. There were, however, eggs which became rotten. It did not matter. People were making omelets from those rotten eggs and were eating those omeletts!

Other Practices and the Diploma Project

My first Practice was after the second year of education at the Mosrybvtuz, at a Shipyard, in the City of Astrakhan', in the Southern Russia. That city is located on the Volga River, not far from the Caspian Sea.

I remember that on the local Farmers Market there was an abundance of tomatoes, wonderful tomatoes of the home-grown quality. The climate of that area is probably very benefitial to growing tomatoes. One could buy black caviar on that Farmers Market, too.

My second Practice was the Sailing Practice (which I decribed in the previous section).

My third Practice was at a Shipyard, in the City of Kiev, in the Ukraine.

My fourth, and the final (the Pre-Diploma) Practice was at a Ship Design Bureau in Klaipeda, a port city on the shore of the Baltic Sea, in Lithuania.

My then wife joined me in Klaipeda. There is a spit in the Baltic Sea, a long narrow piece of land going from some place located to the north of Kaliningrad - to Klaipeda. The name of that spit is the Curonian Spit. To the west of that spit is the Baltic Sea, and to the east is the Curonian Lagoon.

I first learned about that spit and about that lagoon from my father. As I mentioned above in this book, the Army to which my father's artillery unit belonged finished the war (the Second World War) at Konigsberg (which was renamed Kaliningrad in 1946). The name of the Curonian Lagoon in the Lithuanian language is Kursiu Marios, and that is what my father called that lagoon.

We - my wife and I - rented a small room at a place located on the Curonian spit, and that is where we lived during my practice in Klaipeda. The spit was covered by woods. One could enjoy the sun at the beach and swim in the sea on the side of the Baltic Sea of the spit - during the daytime. But not after some hour in the evening, when the frontier guards were in control of the beach ...

I remember the case when we - my wife and I - went to some eatery during that time in Klaipeda. We ordered some Lithuanian dish; what was the name of that dish, I do not remember. We were brought two plates with the dish, and the dish was very tasty. However, on one of the plates, we discovered, in the food, a big bended metal nail.

How did it happen that that nail appeared in the food, I do not know. I do not want to think that somebody put it in the food intentionally. But - who knows.

The three Baltic Countries - Lithuania, Latvia, and Estonia - were for some time (after the communist revolution of 1917 in the Russian Empire and until approximately 1939-1940) independent countries.

And then the Soviet Union invaded these countries. They became Republics in the USSR. They were not independent countries anymore. The native population of these three republics probably looked at us, visitors from Moscow, as representatives of the invaders.

Today, these three Baltic countries are independent countries again, and they can live in the ways they choose to be the best ways of life for them ...

To graduate from Mosrybvtuz, I needed to make and to defend the Diploma Project, the project of a ship. Usually students preferred to do projects of ships similar to the projects which were already done by the previous graduates.

I did not want to do a project of the type which was already done by others. I wanted to do something different. Among the subjects for the Diploma Projects, there was the project of a Self-Propelled Repair Ship for Repair of the Fishing Vessels in the Baltic Sea. Nobody from the previous graduates did such a project. I volunteered to do that project.

The Rukovoditel' (Leading Professor) for that project was the Dean of our Fakul'tet (the Fakul'tet of Shipbuilding) Dotsent (Associate Professor) Foka Antonovich Rozenfeld. Foka Antonovich sounds like a Russian name, but he was not Russian. He was a Jew, and whether Foka Antonovich was his actual name, or that was a Russified version of his actual name - I do not know.

Foka Antonovich was a man of few words. And he was a man of his word, too. He was an excellent Dean. Somebody who cared deeply about his students.

At the age of seventy, or so, our Professor of Structural Mechanics Aleksandr Iosifovich Segal' (whom I already mentioned earlier in this book) lost his vision, and he could not teach us anymore. On his recommendation probably, the Institute hired a new Professor of Structural Mechanics for us. His name was A.S. Vol'mir (Arnol'd Sergeevich

Vol'mir (1910-1986)).

A.S. Vol'mir was a very well-known specialist in the field of Structural Mechanics. He was, I believe, Professor at the Zhukovskii Air Force Engineering Academy in Moscow.

All this was good, but not quite sufficient for our Dean. Our Dean wanted to know firsthand how good Professor Vol'mir was as a teacher. So when Professor Vol'mir was teaching us for the first time, the door to the lecture-hall opened, and our Dean quietly came in. He sat and listened to Professor Vol'mir's lecture for maybe half-an-hour. Then, as quietly as he came, he left the room. Now he knew how good our new Professor was - as a teacher.

Well, since there were no any materials on the project of a Self-Propelled Repair Ship in the archives, I had to do that project from scratch (so to speak). However, Foka Antonovich told me that there was such a ship, a Self-Propelled Repair Ship, moored at that time at the Pregolia (Pregel - in the German language) River, in Kaliningrad, and that I would be given the opportunity to examine that ship.

After Klaipeda, I came to Kaliningrad, and during a couple of days, I examined that ship. That helped me a lot during the time when I was working on my Diploma Project.

Making my project "from scratch," I needed more time than usual to finish the project. One day, when our dean came across me at the Mosrybvtuz, he told me that if I did not defend my Diploma Project in the middle of March (of 1959), I would then need to wait for about one year to defend it. A certain day in the middle of March was the last day to defend diploma projects that year.

In the beginning of February of 1959, my daughter was born. To finish my project on time, I did not sleep some nights. I did defend my Diploma Project in the middle of March (of 1959), and I got "A" for that project.

On the Colors: Green and Red

In the beginning of the previous section, I mentioned tomatoes on the Farmers Market in Astrakhan'. When we - my mother and I - lived in Italy (on the way to the United States), in the city called Lido-di-Ostia, there were tomatoes of two colors on the Farmers Market: green and red. And the price of the green tomatoes was higher than the price of the red tomatoes.

Also, on the subject of colors, green and red. In the food store close to the place where we - my mother, father, and I - lived in Moscow when I was a boy and a teenager, there was a ketchup. That ketchup was of the green color. When we came to the United States, I was surprised to see that ketchup in America is of the red color. I expected it to be, as in that food store in Moscow, of the green color ...

And here is one more thing about colors, green and red. When we - my mother and I - were leaving the USSR, I knew that on the way to the United States we would be living for some time in Italy. So I bought in a bookstore in Moscow two small (pocket-size) dictionaries. One was the Russian-Italian Dictionary, and another one was the Italian-Russian Dictionary.

The dominant color of the cover of one of them was green, with some area of red, and the dominant color of the cover of another one was red, with some area of green. In Italy, for a couple of weeks, I was walking with these two dictionaries in my pockets. After those weeks, I was able to communicate with Italians - somehow - asking simple questions and getting answers.

To my eye, the green and the red colors go well together.

On Teaching

I shall write now about two of my Professors at Mosrybvtuz, Professor A.I. Segal' and Professor Kul'man. They both were good teachers. However, their teaching styles were different.

Professor A.I. Segal' was teaching us Structural Mechanics of the Ship. He was Jewish. Being an erudite in his field, he was sometimes going "to the right or to the left" from the main subject of his lecture. (To the right or to the left, but always staying within the boundaries of Structural Mechanics.)

I liked that, because I was reading the textbook on the subject he taught us - in advance of his lectures. Most of the students, I believe, did not like those excursions to the right or to the left. They were interested - predominantly - to learn things which they would be asked on the final examination.

I liked Professor Segal' teaching very much.

Professor Kul'man was teaching us Physics. He was Swedish. (In Fargo, North Dakota, where I now live, there is, I am sure, a big number of people who are ethnically Swedish. In the Soviet Union, Professor Kul'man was the only Swedish person whom I knew.)

Professor Kul'man was always strictly on the subject of his lecture. Going "to the right or to the left" was not his style.

Moreover, he told us, students, what were the main things we needed to know on the final examination. He called them "Elephants." Elephant Number One, Elephant Number Two, Elephant number Three, etc. That definitely was of help.

I liked Professor Kul'man's teaching too.

One time, I was sitting in the first row, and Professor Kul'man started his lecture. I had a piece of bread with a jam, which I brought from home, and I needed to finish eating it. He looked at me, eating in the beginning of his lecture, and he told, "That is fine. Eat. Because if you are hungry, you will not be able to digest my lecture."

(Professor Kul'man died, I think, at the age of seventy. He was dancing, and something happened to his heart. He needed to be given medicine which was in his pocket. But nobody knew that, and he died. That is what I heard of his death.)

Some of my teachers - at school and at Mosrybvtuz - were rather strict. One time, I was late for the lecture on the Strength of Materials, at Mosrybvtuz.

The lecture has already started, and the door to the lecture-hall was locked. I knocked on the door. Professor teaching us that subject opened the door, and I asked, "May I come in?" "Net," he told, and he shut the door! ("Net" is the Russian word for "Not," as you probably know.)

I think that that strickness came from the pre-revolution (of 1917) times. For example, I heard that in the Russian Empire, if an engineer designed and built (with a team of construction workers) a railroad bridge, then the first time the train was going over that bridge, that engineer had to stand under the bridge, in the middle of it! That is strict!

I recollect my teachers at school and my Professors at Mosrybvtuz with warm feelings ...

One thing I want to add here. The gift for research and the gift for teaching are two different gifts. Some people are excellent researchers but not really good teachers. Some people are excellent teachers but not really good researchers. Some people have both these gifts, and some have neither of them.

When we - my mother and I - lived on the East Coast of the United States, I knew a man who was, like us, a Jewish Refugee from the Soviet Union. By profession, he was an electrical engineer. He was educated in Berlin, Germany, before Hitler came to power in that country.

He told me that his Professor of Physics was Albert Einstein. He told me that every student knew that Albert Einstein was Physicist Number One. He also told me that Albert Einstein was not a good teacher for students.

That man was the only former student of Albert Einstein whom I ever met, and what other former students of Albert Einstein were saying about him as a teacher - I do not know.

Universities, I think, need both professors who excel mostly in research and professors who excel mostly in teaching.

As far as I remember, a number of years ago, the State Board of Higher Education of North Dakota made it possible for the Institutions of Higher Education (of North Dakota) to hire both professors whose main activity would be in research and professors whose main activity would be in teaching.

I believe that that is a very proper thing to do!

On Grades, Grading, and on the Teaching Load in Schools

The grades (for the tests and the examinations) which I quote in this book are not the grades which were used in the USSR, but their American equivalents. In the USSR, the grades were numerical: 5, 4, 3, 2, and 1. (The equvalent American grades are: A, B, C, D, and F, respectively.)

Of those five numerical grades, 5, 4, and 3 were the passing grades, and 2 and 1 were the non-passing ones. For the grade 1, the slang name was "kol" - "stake," in translation into the English language. Since both 2 and 1 were the non-passing grades, there was no practical difference between them. Only - that a teacher or a professor could express his frustration with a particular pupil's or student's work evaluating his performance by "kol."

In the USSR, grading was done differently from how it is done in the USA. In the USA, it is customary to give a certain number of points for any problem solved and to then judge the test work by the total number of points given. In the USSR, a teacher or a professor would indicate (usually using the red pencil or pen) all the mistakes in the test work, and then he would assign that work a certain grade - based on his (teacher's or professor's) judgment on what grade that work deserves.

For a school teacher, the normal teaching load in the USSR was eighteen academic hours per week - in class, at the blackboard. Since schools worked six days per week, my father had to teach, on the average, three hours per day. If he taught more than eighteen hours per week, he was paid additional money for those additional hours. (For the vacation time (in summers), teachers were also paid in the USSR.)

Most of the work of preparation and grading, my father did at home. So I saw my father a considerable amount of time.

By the way, I heard that in Germany the teaching load of a school teacher also was eighteen academic hours per week.

Studying Mathematics on My Own

I studied on my own a big number of mathematics subjects. After deciding which subject to study next, I had to first choose a textbook or a monograph by which to study that subject. For that, I usually looked through several books on the subject - to see which of them I liked most. And then, there was a problem of how to get that book.

In the USSR, the sytem "Books in Print" did not exist. Books were printed in a specified number of copies, and when those copies were sold, the only way to find and to buy that book was in a second-hand bookshop. There were a number of such second-hand bookshops in Moscow. Nevertheless, often I could not find and buy the book which I needed. In such cases, I used books borrowed from libraries.

My way of studying mathematics was what I would call the active study. Looking at a certain theorem, for example, I first tried to understand what exactly the author of the book was proving, and then I tried to prove that theorem on my own. If I had no idea of how to do that, I then read the beginning of the proof in the book, trying to get a hint on how to proceed. I then tried to proceed based on that hint, and if at a certain point in the proof I got stuck, I then glanced at the proof in the book again, trying to get the next hint, etc. That way of study, the active study, worked well for me.

Also, after that my initial (mentioned above in this book) negative experience with Complex Variables, when I was just studying theory without solving problems, in all the subsequent studies of the mathematics subjects, I was solving a considerable number of problems on the subject, some of them of a rather elevated difficulty.

In Reserve of the Soviet Navy

Being a male student at Mosrybvtuz, I had to take military courses. That was something similar, I think, to the ROTC (Reserve Officer Training Corps) in the USA, with that difference that in the USA, participation in that program is voluntary, and in the USSR, it was mandatory. Also, in the USA, both male and female students can take these courses, and at Mosrubvtuz, it was for the male students only.

I do not remember for how many years I had to take those military courses, but at the end of the fourth year of the Institute education, the military courses stopped. We - a group of students - were then taken to some place near the city of Tallin, in Estonia, were given sailor's uniforms, and spent one month in the Soviet Navy. Not at sea, though, but on the shore of the Baltic Sea.

I have no recollection of what we were doing during that month, with one exception. One day, we were given rifles and sent to guard some ammunition depot. We were sent to guard that depot at night. I was standing alone at the place I was assigned to be and could not see any other guards.

If I had to actually use that rifle, I would not know how to use it to fire: nobody taught us that. And, in addition to that, we were not given any cartridges for the rifles!

After that one month in the Navy as seamen, we were assigned the rank of junior lieutenants.

When I was twenty five, I was summoned for one month of service in the Navy again. That time, it was near the city of Riga, in Latvia. We were stationed on the shore of the Baltic sea, that was in summer, and we could sometimes go to the beach and swim. The water was rather cold though.

And we could go sometimes to Riga, dressed in our civilian clothes. Riga is a beautiful city, but all I remember of that city was a restaurant called the Milk Restaurant, nothing else.

After the one-month service near Riga, I was advanced to the rank of lieutenant. Later, I was summoned - two times, I think - to attend military courses at some Moscow Institutes. By the time we left the Soviet Union, I held the rank of senior lieutenant, in Reserve of the Soviet Navy.

Gout

When I was twenty five, I got gout. My gout manifested itself for the first time when I was serving in the Navy near Riga.

This is how that happened. I usually wear wide shoes (3E when I was younger and 4E now), but the boots which I then received from the Navy were, although my size, but too narrow for me. In addition to that, I had to walk a lot on the cobble-stone pavement. After about two weeks of such walking, the big toe of my right foot swelled. I had pain and was limping.

We had a medical doctor in our Navy unit. As I, he was from the Reserve of the Navy. He examined my big toe but could not determine what caused the swelling and the pain. (Well, gout is an arthritis. But rheumatology was very far from the medical specialization of our doctor. He was a gynaecologist.)

In the USSR, gout was a rare disease. My rheumatologist in Moscow for several years did not suspect that I had gout. She thought that I had some bad kind of arthritis (rheumatoid arthritis (?)), and she treated me with penicillin.

Then one day I was seen by a good specialist. A woman - she was Professor at the Institute of Medicine in Moscow - just felt the uppers of my ears with her fingers and told me, "There is a good suspicion that you have gout." The proper blood test was made, and that test confirmed that I did have gout (podagra).

Having gout, one is in a good company. In particular, the famous scientist Isaac Newton (Sir Isaac Newton (1643-1727)) had gout, and the famous Admiral Nelson (Lord Nelson (1758-1805), British Navy Commander) had gout too.

Good medicines for gout the USSR was importing from other countries. There were many pharmacies in Moscow. Some of them could have, on a certain day, an imported medicine which I needed, others might not have it.

One of the pharmacies, in the center (downtown) of Moscow, not far from the Kremlin, was (called) the Central Pharmacy. That pharmacy had the information on which pharmacies in Moscow had specific medicines. To buy a medicine I needed for gout, I had to first call the Central Pharmacy. That pharmacy would tell me whether that medicine was available in Moscow on that day or not. And if it was available, which pharmacy or pharmacies had it.

Concert of a Japanese Jazz-Band

Having the short-wave receivers, I could listen to jazz music, and I liked that music very much. However, until I was twenty-five, I never was at a live concert of a jazz-band.

I grew up in the 1940s and 1950s. I do not think that the Soviet authorities were then fans of the jazz music. There were jazz musicians in the USSR. For example, there was a famous jazz-band of Leonid Utesov. Leonid Utesov (1895-1982) was a Jew and originally from Odessa. (Leonid Utesov was not his actual name but his pseudonym.)

However, jazz was, I believe, not an encouraged-to-perform music at those times in the USSR. The jazz concerts were very rare then. So living in Moscow, where there was a lot of cultural activity, I was in play theaters, in opera, in operetta, in ballet, in symphony concerts, but not in a live concert of a jazz-band - until I was tweny-five, as I just mentioned.

Sometime in 1962, when I was twenty-five, I learned that there were two foreign jazz-bands visiting the USSR and performing in Moscow at the same time. One was the Benny Goodman Orchestra from the United States, and another one was the Hiroshi Watanabe jazz-band from Japan.

By the time I learned that, all tickets to the performances of the Benny Goodman Orchestra in Moscow were sold. But the tickets to the performances of the Hiroshi Watanabe jazz-band were available, and I bought two tickets and attended, together with my then wife, one of the concerts of that band.

That was a memorable experience for me.
Mr. Watanabe, conducting his band, was moving enthusiastically, almost dancing. The music was exceptionally good and cheerful, and the performance of the music was excellent. I remembered that concert - all my life.

Counting Committee

As I mentioned above in this book, when defending my Dissertation, the voting (by the members of the Scientific Council of the Institute for the Problems of Mechanics) was by secret ballot. To count the votes - for, or against - the Counting Committee was created. The Committee consisted of three members.

Well, that Committee definitely had good credentials to count. Two of the members of the Committee were prominent Professors of Mathematics: Professor Mark Iosifovich Vishik, specialist in partial differential equations (later in life he became a Member of the Academy of Sciences of the USSR) and Professor Viktor Borisovich Lidskii, specialist in functional analysis. (Who was the third member of the Committee - I do not remember.)

Remark. *I just wrote that Professor Vishik became, later in life, a Member of the Academy of Sciences of the USSR. Membership in the Academy was by election. Those were the scientists with the highest achievements in their respective fields of science who were elected to be the Members of the Academy.*

There were two categories of the Members of the Academy. The first category was the Corresponding Members, and the second (higher) category was what I would call the Full Members of the Academy.

The Full Member of the Academy was called, in the Russian language, Akademik. The English translation for the Russian word Akademik is Academician.

In this book, if I know that a person was a Full Member of the Academy of Sciences of the USSR, I write that he was Academician.

Scientific Presentations and Falling in Love

As a scientist, I worked alone all my life, and making presentations at scientific meetings or conferences was not a big part of my scientific activity. I made presentations at three such events in the USSR and at four (all of them - Meetings of the American Mathematical Society) in the USA.

Falling in love? That happened very rarely in my life. The first time that happened, I was nineteen, and I married that woman being twenty years of age, and that marriage turned out to be a huge mistake. I divorced her when I was twenty nine, and I never married again after that.

Socks of Different Colors on My Right and Left Feet, Etc.

I was then in my early thirties (or in the mid-thirties maybe), and I was divorced. In the Moscow Metro (the Underground; in the USA, it is called Subway) or on the public transportanion bus maybe, I met a woman, and we agreed to meet again.

We met again and were walking along some street and talking. And I sensed that that woman was a little nervous. I aked her, "Why?"

She then told me that it was announced on the radio that a prisoner escaped from a prison in the area where we were walking, and that that prisoner had socks of different colors on his right and left feet. I looked at my feet, and to my astonishment, I discovered that the socks on my right and left feet were of different colors! So my date had the reason to be nervous!

We, that woman and I, had one more date after that. During that date, the woman, not realizing (?) that I am a Jew, suddenly started sharing with me her anti-semitic feelings. I then immediately told her that I am a Jew. That was the end of our dating.

That was not the first time when such a thing happened. When I was seventeen, after I finished my first year as a student at Mosrybvtuz, in the summer of 1954, my parents and I were on vacation in some resort city on the shore of the Black Sea. (What city that was, I do not remember.) At the place where we stayed, we had neighbours, a husband and wife, and they had a daughter, a little younger than I then was. I invited that daughter on a date.

I remember that we - that girl and I - were sitting on a bench in a park on the shore of the sea and talking. On some reason, the name of the city of Odessa was mentioned. And then that girl told me that she did not like the city of Odessa, because there were "too many Jews" in that city. When I told her that I am a Jew, she started to apologize. That was the end of our dating, too.

The two cases which I just described took place in the USSR. And now I shall describe the case of a similar nature, and that happened in Fargo, North Dakota, USA.

I was then forty eight (or forty nine maybe), and at the Singles Dances, I met a woman. During a few such Dances, we were dancing together sometimes, and we were talking. And then that woman invited me to come to her family Christmas celebration. I thanked her for the invitation and told that I would be glad to come. That was a good opportunity for me to meet her parents and her relatives.

Between the Christmas day and that Dance, there was one more occasion of the Singles Dances. On the day of those Dances, I mentioned to that woman that I am a Jew.

She did not hesitate a second to respond. My invitation to her family Christmas celebration was immediately cancelled. Unpleasantly surprised, I asked her, "Why?" "Christmas is for Christians," she answered. That was the end of our dancing together and of our conversations.

I do not want to think that the cases which I just described are typical. Maybe they are the exceptions. But that is what happened to me, on three occasions.

Long Vacation

Some time after we, my mother and I, submitted our applications for the exit visas from the USSR, there was a letter in our mailbox. I could see that that letter was from the local Voenkomat. (Voenkomat is an abbreviation for Voennyi Komissariat, in translation into English - Military Commissariat.) That could only mean trouble. So I did not even touch that letter.

At the place where I worked at that time, I accumulated a considerable time of unused vacations. I immediately came to my superior at work and told him that I wanted to use my vacation time.

I did not tell at my work that I applied for the exit visa from the USSR, but they definitely knew that. They were glad to get rid of me - for some time at least - and I was quickly given the permission to use my vacation time. I bought the train ticket and left Moscow.

I remember that I went to Sevastopol', in the Crimea, then (maybe, this I do not remember precisely) to Yalta, also in the Crimea, then to Odessa, on the Black Sea, then to Rybnitsa, in Moldavia (the place where my father was born), and, finally, to Chernovtsy, in the (Western) Ukraine. In Odessa, Rybnitsa, and Chernovtsy, our family had relatives or friends, and I told them that we, my mother and I, wanted to leave the USSR.

When I came back to Moscow, my mother told me that a man from the Voenkomat called and asked where I was, and she told him that I was on vacation.

Soon after I returned to Moscow, a letter came from OVIR, stating that we were granted the exit visas and telling that I (or we) should come at a certain day to the Central Office of OVIR to receive those visas. Also, my mother and I had to pay five hundred Soviet roubles each (a large amount of money, relative to the salaries in the USSR) to cease to be the Soviet citizens.

We paid the money, received the exit visas, and were not the Soviet citizens anymore. Suddenly, the man from the Voenkomat called again. It turned out that the Voenkomat wanted me to attend some courses at the Moscow State University, for military preparation. I think that if I attended those courses, they would then tell that I know some military secrets and would deny me the exit visa.

I told that man that I was not the Soviet citizen anymore. "Do you have the exit visa?" he aked. "Yes," I told. At that moment, it was too late for the Voenkomat to do anything. We were free to leave the USSR ...

By the way, when we - my mother and I - were not the Soviet citizens anymore, but before we left the USSR, there were elections. On a certain day, the entire country was supposed to go to the polls.

Of course, those were the Soviet elections. There was

only one candidate for every position, and that candidate was chosen by the Government - to be the candidate. So those elections were always simply a farce.

Being not the Soviet citizens anymore, my mother and I were not supposed to vote. So we were glad not to go to the voting place on that day. Suddenly, in the late afternoon (or in the early evening maybe), there was a knock on the door of our apartment. A man came from that voting place and asked us to go to vote. We explained to him that we were not Soviet citizens anymore and that we were not supposed to vote.

Please, he told us, go and vote. Your names are on the list of people who are supposed to vote, and you are the last ones who did not vote yet. "If you go and vote," he told, "I shall be able to go home then." Well, to make it possible for that man to go home, we went and voted. We knew that those elections were only a farce ...

Engineering Computations

In my lifetime, I witnessed a complete change in how engineering computations were made.

When I studied engineering, the engineers in the USSR were using slide-rules to make computations. We, students, used slide-rules too. I still have one (of two) slide-rules which I used when I was studying engineering. The length of the working part of that instrument is twenty five centimeters (about 9.8 inches), and the total length of the instrument is a little less than twenty eight centimeters (about 11 inches). Such a slide-rule was able to give the results of computations with the precision of three digits (of mantissa). For example, it could give the result 0.924, but not 0.9243. For the most of the engineering computations, such precision was sufficient.

Later, I had fifty-centimeters-long slide-rule, which was capable of giving the results of computations with the precision of four digits.

When I entered Aspirantura, I first used the electro-mechanical computing machines. These were heavy, made from metal table devices, which, when working, were producing considerable noise: dy-dy-dy- ... . The advantage of these machines was that they were capable of giving the results of computations with the precision of seven or eight digits, and that was a huge improvement comparing to the precision of the slide-rules.

At a certain moment - at the end of 1963 or in the beginning of 1964 maybe - Professor Gurevich told me that a certain engineering department of MIIT had a computer, and that I could use that computer. As all the computers of that time, that was a mainframe computer. It used not the usual for computers system "zero and one" but the system "zero, minus one, and plus one."

The programming for that computer had to be made in machine commands, and a ribbon had to be prepared, with the rows of punched or not punched holes. Each row had five places for the holes to be punched. I learned the beginnings of such programming and was able to prepare the necessary for my computations ribbon without mistakes. (If I made mistakes, I would not know how to correct them, other than making a different ribbon.)

I had to make computations for a number of different cases (for my problem) using that computer. For three (probably) of these cases, I made computations using the electro-mechanical machines, and when I received the same results for those cases using the computer, I knew that my ribbon was prepared correctly.

That was the first time that I used a computer.

Later, I used different computers, where cards with holes in them had to be prepared for computations. When I worked at the Institute for the Problems of Mechanics of the Academy of Sciences of the USSR, they had what was called BESM - The Large Electronic Computing Machine, the most powerful computer the USSR had at that time (as far as I know). The BESM was on tubes, and it occupied a considerable space. I used that computer, and for that I learned the beginnings of the computing language called Fortran.

In the USSR, I never had a calculator.

In the USA, at my first job, at a small Research and Development Company on the East Coast, I used a calculator (a programmable calculator) for the first time in my life. However, it was much more convenient to use a computer for the computations I had to make. The computer which I could use was at some University on the West Coast of the USA, and I had to learn the programming language Super Fortran (that is how that language was called, as far as I remember).

After maybe three days of learning Super Fortran, I was able to make a program and to make computations which I had to make. The communications with that computer, on the West Coast, were using the telephone line.

My first personal computer I bought in 1997, when I was working at the Valley City State University. I also bought Mathematica, a computing software, and it worked well for me.

I just mentioned that in the USSR I never had a calculator.

There were things of which I never even heard when I lived in the USSR. For example, the scotch tape. I first saw the scotch tape when we - my mother and I - were on the train from Vienna, Austria, to Rome, Italy, in 1977. Our names were written on the scotch tape, and that tape was then attached to our luggage.

Another thing about which I never heard when I lived in the USSR was the correction fluid - to correct typing mistakes. (Well, not many people in the USSR had typewrites in any case. When I had to fill in the applications for the exit visas, I had to rent a typewriter, for a few days, from some renting store in Moscow.)

I never owned a stapler in the USSR. But at my last job, one day, a stapler appeared. Having no experience with a stapler before, I contrived to drive staple into one of my fingers. Not the most pleasant experience that was ...

And now, recalling that train from Vienna to Rome, in 1977. Everybody in our passenger car was a Jewish Refugee from the Soviet Union. And to protect us, the armed guards were placed in the entrances to our car.

How I Gambled and Lost Money in Las Vegas

In January of 1997, I came to San Diego, California, to make a presentation at the 103rd Annual Meeting of the American Mathematical Society. The way back, from San Diego to Fargo, was by me using the Greyhound bus lines.

The bus had stops at different cities, and one of the stops was in Las Vegas. We, the passengers, were told that the bus needed maintanance and that the duration of the stop in Las Vegas would be two hours. So I was walking along some street, in the vicinity of the bus depot, and I saw a place with gambling machines. I came inside and decided to put some money in one of those machines.

I put my hand in the pocket of my trousers and found one-cent coin. I put that coin in the machine and lost it. I then put my hand in the same pocket and found five-cents coin. I put that coin in the same machine and lost it too. I then put my hand in that pocket again and found ten-cents coin. That was the last coin in that pocket.

And then I told myself, "If you put this ten-cents coin in the machine and lose it, then you are a gambler!" "No," I told myself, "I do not want to be a gambler!" And instead of putting that ten-cents coin in the machine, I put it back in my pocket.

And now I can tell that I did gamble in Las Vegas, and I lost money. In the amount of six cents.

And I proved to myself that I am not a gambler!

My Bowling Experience

There were a number of the bus stops on that way from San Diego, California, to Fargo, North Dakota. After the bus arrived at Dickinson, North Dakota, for a day the bus could not go any further: there was a blizzard, and the highway I-94 (leading from Dickinson to Fargo) was closed.

In the place where the bus station in Dickinson was, there

were an eatery (a cafe or a restaurant maybe) and a bowling place. I never tried bowling before that. Living in the USSR, I never even heard of bowling.

(Well, living in the USSR, I never heard of many things American. For example, living in the USSR, I did not know that there are the North Dakota State and the South Dakota State in the USA. I did know, however, that at the time of the Second World War, there was a military transport airplane in the USA called Dakota. So I thought that Dakota was the name of the airplane. It was only sometime after my mother and I came to the USA that I learned that there are the North Dakota and the South Dakota States in the country.)

I decided to try to bowl. Rented, for a dollar, the bowling shoes, took a ball in my hands, and tried to throw it. What I discovered was that it was difficult for me to throw the ball when I was moving. I had to stop first and to throw the ball after that. I am glad that I tried to bowl then in Dickinson. It was - my only bowling experience.

Crossing USA by Bus

That trip, by bus, from San Diego, California, to Fargo, North Dakota, was only one of the bus trips which I had during my life in the USA.

When my mother and I lived on the East Coast, once I was invited for an interview visit to a place near Chicago. The people who invited me expected me to come by plane, and they were surprised when I told them that I prefer to come by bus. The reason for me choosing the bus was very simple: I wanted to see my new country, and for that the bus is much better than the airplane.

In totality, I crossed the United States by bus (using the Greyhound and other similar bus lines) from the East Coast to the West Coast, and from the North (Fargo, North Dakota) to the South (Denton, Texas). I was in Denton in 1999, attending the Fourth International Meeting of the American Mathematical Society and of the Sociedad Matematica Mexicana. I came to make a presentation at that meeting.

I am glad that I crossed the United States by bus. A number of places which I saw during those trips are in my memory.

About Some Cities Where I Was

I was in a number of cities. In the USSR, in Austria, in Italy, in the USA, and in Israel.

The city where I was born, Kamenets-Podolsk, I do not remember. I was only two-and-a-half years old when my family moved from Kamenets-Podolsk to Moscow. And - I never returned to that city.

Of many cities where I was or lived, I do have memories. Here, I shall share with the reader some of my memories connected to some of those cities.

Vladivostok, in the USSR (today - city in the Russian Federation). In that city I was in 1956, on the way to the Sea of Okhotsk. Vladivostok was the base for the Far-East Navy of the USSR. And although I was the Soviet Citizen, it was not possible for me to come to Vladivostok without a special permission from the Soviet Government.

It was the Mosrubvtuz that sent me (and several other

students) to the Sea of Okhotsk. The Mosrybvtuz bought the train tickets for us. However, first they had to apply for the permission for us to come to Vladivostok. Without such a permission, the train station would not sell the train tickets to Vladivostok.

Leningrad, in the USSR (today - Saint Petersburg in the Russian Federation). I was in Leningrad two times. One time - to attend a Conference, where I made a presentation on the subject of the Jet Curtain of an Air-Cushion Vehicle. Another time - on a personal reason. On both occasions, I did not have much time to see the treasures of that city.

From what I saw, I was impressed by the Hermitage, one of the biggest and the finest art museums in the world, by the Russian Museum, a museum of the Russian art, and by the Saint Isaac's Cathedral, a Cathedral of the Russian Orthodox Church.

Tallin, in Estonia, the USSR (today - the capital of the independent country Estonia). Tallin has a very interesting Old Town (a medieval city).

Naftalan, in Azerbaijan, the USSR (today - city in the independent country Azerbaijan). That is a small city. Naftalan is also the name of a special kind of oil (some kind of young oil) which is used to treat patients with some ilnesses. The City of Naftalan has a facility to treat patients with that oil.

The patients take baths filled with the oil, and they are instructed to keep their hearts above the level of the oil - when in baths. After such a bath, it is not easy to wash off the oil from the body. Taking such a bath is a rather exhaustive procedure.

Moscow, the capital of the USSR (today - the capital of the Russian Federation). Moscow was the largest cultural center in the USSR. I will mention here two museums in Moscow: The Trtetyakov Gallery, a gallery of the Russian fine art, and The Pushkin Museum, a museum of the European art. I was in each of them several times.

One time, there was an exhibition of paintings by the French Impressionists in the Pushkin Museum. I visited that exhibition three times. One time by myself, one time with my parents, and one time with my then girlfriend.

Vienna, in Austria. Vienna was the first city outside the USSR where my mother and I were. We lived in Vienna for two days. The city was extremely clean. It was making an impression of a "model of the order."

Lido di Ostia, in Italy. Lido di Ostia is a small pleasant city on the shore of the Terranian Sea, about thirty minutes by train from Rome. My mother and I lived in that city, on the way to the United States, for about two-and-a-half months. When we arrived in Italy, we first lived, for two weeks, in Rome. That was in July (of 1977). It was hot in Rome, and the air was filled, to some extent, with fumes of the gasoline.

After those two weeks, we moved to Lido di Ostia. There was always a cool breeze from the sea there. There was a park on the shore of the sea in Lido di Ostia, and that was a nice place to spend time.

From time to time, we were coming from Lido di Ostia to Rome. Sometimes the train to Rome was not going. That was happening when somebody called the train station and told that there was a bomb on the track. Well, that never happened to be true, but in the meantime, the train was not going, and the passengers had to wait at the train station until the railway service was restored.

The New York City, in the USA. The New York City is probably the largest cultural center in the USA. At the time when we - my mother and I - lived in New York, or close to New York, there were about one hundred museums in the city. I was in about two dozen of them. Mostly, with my mother, in some of them - alone, and in some of them - with my then girlfriend.

My mother and I were one time in the Metropolitan Opera, two-three times in the New York City Opera, a couple of times in the Carnegie Hall, and one time in the performance of the New York City Ballet.

Annapolis, in the USA. For me, Annapolis was the most pleasant city. It is situated on the Chesapeake Bay. It is the city where the United States Naval Academy is located. Annapolis was the place where I had my first, temporary job in the USA. We - my mother and I - lived in Annapolis for about four months. I was in the Library of the Naval Academy and borrowed some mathematics books from that library. I liked Annapolis a lot.

Jerusalem, in Israel. In Jerusalem, every building is reveted with a white stone from the hills in the vicinity of the city. When looking at Jerusalem from the hills, on a sunny day, the entire city shines!

We - my mother and I - spent about four days in Jerusalem (when visiting Israel in the summer of 1987). That summer was very-very hot. It was very humid in Tel-Aviv, which is located at sea level. Jerusalem is only about forty five minutes by bus from Tel-Aviv, but it is about 757 meters (2484 feet) above sea level. It was also hot in

Jerusalem, but it was dry, not humid.

On the Internet, one can find a wealth of information about the cities which I just mentioned. My goal here was modest: to share with the reader *some of my specific memories* of those cities.

On the Matter of Food

My father told me once, with a smile, "Some people eat to live, and some people live to eat."

Those are the extremes, of course. However, people definitely want their food to be tasty. But what is tasty and what is not tasty - may be different for people from different cultures.

When I was in my thirties, I read a book written by some American author. It was the Russian translation of that book. What that book was about and who was that author, I do not remember. I do remember, however, that it was written in that book that the Russians think that when the Americans make food, they just spoil good products. And that the Americans think that when the Russians make food, they just spoil good products.

Whether that is right or not, I do not know. And even if that is right, that cannot be right entirely. I am sure, there are many American dishes and many Russian dishes which *people of both these nations* would find tasty. However, there is definitely a substantial difference between these two cuisines.

I think that our taste is developed when we are small children and teenagers. Coming to a different country, where people eat foods different from the foods which you were normally eating, can create a problem for a person. When I had to be, for a period of several months, in a hospital and in two nursing homes, the food which I could get in two of those establishments was a problem for me.

That was a very good and definitely a very nutritious food, which they were serving. But that food was tailored to the taste of somebody who was raised in America, and my taste was different. I had a difficult time trying to find the dishes which I would have an appetite to eat. When you are ill, often you have little appetite for food, in any case ...

In the third of these establishments, a nursing home, on the day I was brought to that place, somebody from their kitchen came and asked me, "What dishes do you eat?" I named a few very simple dishes, very easy to prepare, and told them that I was ready to eat these dishes every day. And - they were cooking these dishes for me, and I was eating them! That helped me a lot!

Chapter 4

Some Events In The Lives Of My Grandparents And Parents.

More About My Grandparents

My paternal grandmother, Enia Tsel'nik, I never saw. She died when she was forty nine years old. My parents were then in high school. I have two photographs of my grandmother Enia. In one of them, she is alive, and in another one - she is dead.

My paternal grandfather, Shlema (Shlomo) Tsel'nik, I saw. He came to visit our family, my father, my mother, and me, in Moscow, sometime before the Second World War. That probably was in 1940 or in 1941. Being then of age three or four maybe, I do not have a clear memory of his visit. With the exception that I do have a certain picture in my mind - of him approaching the place where we then lived. That was the only time in my life that I saw him.

Shlema Tsel'nik was a very kind man. When my mother and father told him that they would marry, he promised to give them, as a wedding gift, a thing from gold (a watch maybe?) which he had.

However, his neighbors' son got ill, and the family needed money for their son's treatment. Or maybe the money was necessary to send that son to some place for a treatment. The neighbours, however, did not have the necessary money. My grandfather Shlema then gave the neighbours that golden thing (and my father and mother did not receive that thing as a wedding gift).

My grandfather Shlema Tsel'nik died sometime during the Second World War. At the time of his death, he was, I think, in his mid-sixties.

My maternal grandparents I knew very well.

My mathernal grandmother, Hana Spivak (Hana Grossman was her maiden name, Anna Izrailevna Spivak, by her Soviet documents), was the youngest child in her family, the twenty third child! So she had twenty two brothers and sisters! (I never heard of a bigger number of children in a family!)

At the time she was born (in 1878), her father worked as a manager of a big agricultural estate of a wealthy landowner. Hana's father was paid very well, and so her parents had money.

My grandmother Hana (in our family, we called her, tenderly, Hanele) told me that being a child, she saw her mother three times a day. In the morning, at the breakfast time, children kissed mother's hand, in the mid-day, at the dinner time, children kissed mother's hand, and in the evening, at the time of supper, children kissed mother's hand again. All the care of the children was in the hands of other people, who were hired for this purpose, to take care of children.

When my grandmother Hana was a young adult, there was a young Jewish man who wanted to marry her. It was customary at those times for the parents of the bride to give the groom a dowry. However, by that time, the parents of my grandmother Hana were no longer wealthy, and they did not have the money to give as a dowry.

That young Jewish man then told my grandmother, "Hana, I love you, and I would want to marry you. However, if I am not given a dowry, I shall not be able to open a business, and we will not be able to survive." So he did not marry her. Instead, he left for America, and my grandmother never heard of him again.

Being a young woman, my grandmother Hana lived in Warsaw, the capital of Poland. (Poland was then a part of the Russian Empire.) Hana Grossman had a small shop making women's hats, wonderful women's hats of those times.

My maternal grandfather, Ovsei Davidovich Spivak, lived and worked somewhere in Belorussia (also a part of the Russian Empire; Belorussia and Poland were the neighboring parts of that Empire). Somebody introduced Ovsei and Hana to each other. My grandfather Ovsei told me that before he met my grandmother Hana in person, he had a dream in his sleep, and in that dream he saw a face of a woman, and when he met Hana - that was the same face that he saw in his dream!

They married, at twenty eight (they both were of the same age), and settled in the city of Belostok, Poland. My grandfather Ovsei was a new person in that city. He got a job of bukhgalter (this is the name of his profession in the Russian language; in translation into English, that means accountant or book-keeper) at some business, and some salary.

In a short period of time, the owner of that business came to him and told, "Ovsei Davidovich, when I assigned you your salary, I did not know you as a worker. Now I know how you work. I think that for the salary I assigned to you, you will not be working for me for a long period of time. Let me offer you a different salary." And he offered my grandfather Ovsei a better salary. As far as I remember, my grandfather mentioned the sum of one hundred Russian rubles per month, and that happened in 1906 (or so).

That probably was a very good salary for his profession at that time, since my grandfather Ovsei mentioned that sum, one hundred rubles per month, with a visible satisfaction.

Ovsei and Hana had children. Ovsei was working, and Hana was taking care of children and of the household, and she also had a help - a hired woman was coming to help her.

My grandfather Ovsei told me how he was working. He was going to work in the morning, then coming home at the dinner (mid-day) time, and after the dinner, he was sleeping (for an hour maybe). Then, refreshed, he was going to work again. When coming home in the evening, Hana was waiting for him with supper.

One day, when he came home in the evening, after work, Hana was not at home, but that hired woman was, and she told him, "Ovsei Davidovich, your wife prepared supper for you, and now I shall serve you that supper." "And where is my wife?" asked my grandfather. "Oh," answered the woman, "she went to visit her woman-friend."

"My wife did not wait for me to come home after work, to give me the supper?" told my grandfather. "I shall not eat that supper!" And he went to a restaurant and had supper at that restaurant. After that case, my grandmother Hana was always at home in the evening, waiting for her husband to come home after work, to give him the supper. Well, those were different times and different customs.

In 1914, when the First World War started and the German troops were advancing, the family, Ovsei, Hana, and children, moved to Odessa.

In 1917, when the family lived in Odessa, the communist revolution took place. My grandfather Ovsei did not like the new authorities. He called them "bosiakes" (bosiaki - vagabonds, in an approximate translation into English).

My mother was seven, close to eight, when the revolution took place. The communists organized what they called the Red Army, and the people who supported the Tsar' had the White Army, and there was a civil war. In Odessa, the soldiers of one of these Armies were shooting the captured soldiers of another Army. I believe, my mother either saw that or knew about that from other people.

The new authorities introduced the new rules. For example, a family could have not more than a certain number of pillows, depending on the number of people in the family. The representatives of the new authorities were going from apartment to apartment, confiscating the "excess" pillows ...

....

At the end of their lives, my grandparents Ovsei and Hana lived in Moscow. My grandfather Ovsei lived eighty three years. He got emphysema, which was a result of him smoking tobacco-pipe all his adult life. I do not think that at that time the negative effects of smoking tobacco were understood, or fully understood. The emphysema killed him.

My grandmother Hana had a talent: everybody who knew her, liked her. Everybody - young and old - wanted to be in her company. She was the best cook I knew. She could do many things. One day, when they lived in Odessa and my mother was a teenager, there was some event at the school where my mother was a pupil. To come to that event, my mother needed a proper dress, and she did not have one. My grandmother Hana took a drape from the window, worked all night, and in the morning my mother had a dress to come to that event.

My grandmother Hana lived ninety five years. Among her photographs which I have, I have her photograph where she is ninety years of age. I do not see any grey hair in that her photo. And I believe that my grandmother Hana did not use anything to color her hair. At the age of ninety, she went alone, by train, from Moscow to Odessa, to visit her friends in Odessa. Of course, we came with her to the train station in Moscow, and her friends were at the train station in Odessa when her train arrived.

Grandmother Hana told me once that she would never marry a scientist. I asked her, "Why?" "Oh," she told, "every time I come I see you working at your desk. What kind of life would it be for your wife?" (By the way, my father called me "a work-loving bee." I indeed like to work ...)

One more thing I would like to add here. I mentioned that when working in Belostok, my grandfather Ovsei was coming home for dinner in the middle of the day, eating dinner, and then sleeping an hour before going back to work. When I was serving in the Navy, for one month, near Riga, our schedule in the middle of the day was similar. After dinner, we were sleeping for one hour, and then, refreshed, we were going back to performing our duties. Whether in the Russian Navy the schedule is similar today, I do not know.

Story of a Destroyed Dream

My grandfather Ovsei had a special reason not to like the Soviet communists: they destroyed his dream!

As I mentioned above, my grandfather Ovsei (Ovsei Davidovich Spivak) was a bukhgalter (accountant, book-keeper). But - he had a dream: to be a stockbroker. The matter was that he lived in Odessa, and there was no Stock Exhange in Odessa. The Stock Exchange in the Russian Empire was in Saint Petersburg. However, being a Jew, my grandfather was not allowed to live in St. Petersburg!

That is because in the Russian Empire, the Jews were allowed to live only in what was called the Pale of Settlement. And St. Petersburg, the Capital of the Empire, and some other big cities (Moscow, for example) were not in that Pale.

There were some exceptions from that rule. The Jews who had Higher Education (University Education), for example, were allowed to live outside the Pale of Settlement. The Jews who were the very wealthy merchants were allowed to live outside the Pale of Settlement. And there were some other exceptions. However, my grandfather Ovsei did not belong to any of these "exceptional" categories of Jews. So he was not allowed to live in St. Petersburg.

That all changed on the 2nd of April of 1917. There was no Pale of Settlement after that day! (On this matter, see https://en.wikipedia.org/wiki/Pale_of_Settlement.) So my grandfather Ovsei was preparing to move his family to St. Petersburg and to become a stockbroker.

And then, in October of 1917, the communist revolution took place in Russia. And the communists - closed the Stock Exchange! So my grandfather Ovsei never had an opportunity to become a stockbroker!

The Soviet communists destroyed his dream!

The Soviet communists also destroyed the livelihood of my grandfather Shlema (Shlomo Tsel'nik). After the communist revolution of 1917, he had no store anymore (and what was his occupation after that, and until 1942 or 1943 maybe, when he died, I do not know).

My Mother Originally Wanted To Become a Medical Doctor

First of all, I need to explain that the way of educating medical doctors in the USSR was different from the way of educating medical doctors in the USA.

In the USA, after the high school, a person goes to a College, or to a University, and receives his Bachelor's degree. Only after that he goes to study, for four years, medicine and receives the diploma of a medical doctor.

In the USSR, if one wanted to be educated as a medical doctor, he had to go, after the high school, to an Institute of Medicine. The duration of education in such Institutes was six years, during which years students studied medicine, and they also studied all the necessary subjects from other disciplines - simultaneously.

So my mother wanted to become a medical doctor. She could not apply for admission to an Institution of Higher Education immediately after the high school, however.

The rule in the Soviet Union at that time was that if she were a daughter of the working-class parents (of the blue-collar workers), she would be allowed to apply for admission to such an institution immediately after the high school. However, her father being a bukhgalter, he was not a blue-collar worker. In such a case, the authorities required his daughter to earn some experience of work first. So immediately after the high school, my mother worked at some factory, earning her working experience by stitching buttons to shirts.

After she earned the required working experience, my mother submitted her documents to one of the Institutes of Medicine, and she was admitted. On the first day of studies, all the students of her group were taken to the morgue. My mother told me that she went to the morgue with students of her group, turned one hundred eighty degrees, ran to the Rector (Head) of the Institute, and told him, "Please, give me my documents back." The Rector tried to persuade her to stay. He told her, "You have a kind heart, you will be a good doctor." "Not," told my mother, "I cannot stand looking at dead people." And she took her documents back. As I mentioned above in this book, she eventually became an economist.

This shows that the profession of a medical doctor, although being a wonderful profession, is not for everybody. I myself, when I was young, never thought of becoming a medical doctor. Today, I maybe thought differently. However, if I had to become a medical doctor, I would not want to become a physician, a surgeon, or even a cardiologist. I would then want to become a psychiatrist.

For a Period of Time, My Mother Wanted To Become a Translator

When my mother was a girl, her mother, my grandmother Hana, hired a woman who knew English, French, and German languages, and from that woman my mother learned some English, some French, and some German. My mother also learned how to sing the American anthem, in English, from that woman.

My grandfather Ovsei, Hana's husband, did not like the idea of hiring that woman. It is not that he was against education.To the contrary, he was very much for education. He told me once, "They can take almost anything from you. They can take your money, your clothes, your possessions. One thing they cannot take from you - your education." However, the time was hard (that probably was some time after the communist revolution of 1917 in Russia), and my grandfather Ovsei thought that money would be spent better - for buying food. My grandmother Hana insisted, however, and that woman was hired.

When my mother was a student (after the high school), at a certain moment she decided that the profession of translator (interpreter) from English into Russian and from Russian into English would be a good profession for her.

For two years she then studied, in Kiev (then - the capital of the Ukrainian Republic, and today - the capital of Ukraine), the English language, at the Institute the acronym of whose name was UILO. The full name of that Institute was probably Ukrainskii Institute Lingvisticheskogo Obrazovania, in translation into English - the Ukrainian Institute for the Linguistic Education.

On the way from the USSR to the USA, we lived, for a

couple of days, in Vienna, Austria. Using her German, my mother could communicate with people in Vienna. When we came to Rome, Italy, for a couple of weeks we lived at a place the owner of which, a woman, knew French. My mother could communicate with that woman in French.

Perhaps I first heard the sounds of the English language from my mother. I do remember that she was singing a portion of the American anthem, in English, to me.

Lack of Food

In the years when my father and mother were students (after the high school), my father in Odessa, and my mother in Moscow, Kiev, and then in Odessa, they did not have enough food to eat. I do not know what the reason for that was, maybe there was not enough food in the country in those years, or maybe my parents did not have enough money to buy food, or maybe - both.

My father, for a period of time, was then working for the organization called Torgsin. Torgsin is an abbreviation, and the full name of that organization was Torgovlia S Inostrantsami, in translation into English - Trade With Foreigners.

How exactly all this worked, I do not know, but probably the Soviet Citizens who had things of value, such as things made from gold, or from silver, etc., could sell those things to Torgsin, and in return they could buy from Torgsin food, or goods which were not available to the general population.

Working for that organization, my father was able to get some additional food. He was hungry, but he was sending parcels with food to my mother, his future wife, to Moscow, and then to Kiev.

When my parents started their working lives in Kamenets-Podolsk, after they got their Diplomas of Higher Education, all that changed. After years of going hungry, they were able to buy and to eat as much food as they needed.

Voenkomat and the Pregnancy of My Mother

When my parents lived in Kamenets-Podolsk, one day my father received a letter from the Voenkomat. Father was supposed to be drafted, for a certain period of time (for several months maybe?), for the military training. According to the law, however, Father would be excused and not drafted if his wife is pregnant.

The matter was that my mother tried to get pregnant for a few years after my parents married, but she could not. Not thinking that she was pregnant, my mother nevertheless went to her doctor and asked him to check her for pregnancy. She came back home and told my father, "Guess what, I am pregnant!"

That child was me!

Spy in the Hat!

Sometime after the war between Germany and the USSR started, but before my father was drafted into the Soviet Army, once he was standing at a streetcar stop, waiting for his streetcar to come. There was a crowd of people also waiting for their streetcars to come at that stop. My father was in a hat. Other people were either in kepies, or probably with their heads uncovered. Suddenly, a person in that crowd had an idea. "That guy in the hat," he told, pointing at my father, "is a German spy!"

The crowd became agitated. I do not know what the outcome of this agitation could have been, but fortunately there was one person in that crowd who knew who my father was. "Wait a minute," he said, "this man in the hat is the director of our school!" And the crowd immediately calmed down.

Well, that was the Soviet Union soon after the war started, and the idea that there were German spies in the country was probably very much alive.

Two War Front Experiences of My Father

As I mentioned above, my father was drafted into the Soviet Army soon after the invasion of the German Army into the Soviet Union in 1941. At that time, he was the director of one of the Moscow schools. A short time after he was drafted, a new law came into effect - that the directors of schools should not be drafted. However, Father was already in the army (where he spent the next four-and-a-half years of his life).

Here are two of his war front experiences. Once (when he was serving as a field telephonist, I believe) he was sent to the headquarters of his unit, with some message. That was in the nighttime, and he had to walk in a field. Germans were shelling that field. From time to time, German shells were exploding here and there. It was dark, and Father could not find the headquarters. He then laid on the ground and fell asleep. In the morning, when he opened his eyes, he could see the headquarters and was able to deliver his message.

Father was not wounded in the war. Once, when he was in artillery, he bended to lift a shell from the ground, to put it into the gun. He was then in a padded jacket. Suddenly, he felt warmth in the area of his spine. When he took the jacket off, he saw a piece of metal, a piece of the German shell, in the padding of his jacket. If Father were not bended but standing straight, that piece of metal would probably have killed him. Fortunately, he was bended.

One of the consequences of Father's serving in artillery was that his hearing in one of his ears was damaged.

Many men did not return home from that war. We - my mother and I - were extremely lucky. My father returned home.

Chapter 5

Stories About Other People

Professor M.I. Gurevich, a Jew, Was Born in Moscow, Russia, in 1909

My Rukovoditel' at Aspirantura (Leading Professor; in the USA: Ph.D. Adviser), Professor Maksim Isidorovich Gurevich, was born in Moscow, in 1909. For a Jew (both his parents were Jewish), that was unusual. Because Moscow, as I have already mentioned above in this book, was outside the Pale of Settlement in the Russian Empire.

The matter was that his parents, both of them, had Higher Education. His father was an engineer, and his mother was a dentist (educated in France, as far as I know). So, although Jewish, they had the right to live in Moscow (in the Russian Empire).

Professor V.V. Stepanov's Advice

It has been already mentioned in this book that Maksim Isidorovich Gurevich was educated at the Moscow State University.

One of his professors at the University was V.V. Stepanov (Viacheslav Vasil'evich Stepanov (1889-1950)), Professor of Mathematics, specialist in Mathematical Analysis; later in life, he was a Member of the Academy of Sciences of the USSR.

What I am writing about now happened in the 1930 or in

the 1931, in the last academic year of student Maksim Gurevich's education at the University. The matter was that Maksim Gurevich's father was then under arrest. He was arrested by the NKVD.

NKVD is the acronym for Narodnyi Komissariat Vnutrennikh Del, in translation into English - the People's Commissariat for Internal Affairs. NKVD included a predecessor of the KGB.

Somehow, Professor V.V. Stepanov knew that student Maksim Gurevich's father was under arrest. One day, when Professor Stepanov came across student Maksim Gurevich at the University, he told him, "I would like to give you a piece of advice. Do not wait until the scheduled time of the final examinations. Take the final examinations for all the subjects you are studying, now, as soon as you can. If you take and pass all the final examinations, the University will be then obligated to give you your Diploma. Otherwise, nobody knows what can happen."

At that time, a student of the Moscow University could take the final examinations at any time, when he was ready to take them. He only needed to come to his Professor who was teaching him a certain subject and to ask to be examined.

Student Maksim Gurevich followed Professor V.V. Stepanov's advice, took all the final examinations before their scheduled time, and received his Diploma.

Judging by this case, Professor V.V. Stepanov was a good man. And - he was a courageous man too: if the NKVD learned about his advice, he could be in trouble ...

The people who were arrested by the NKVD were all

interrogated, and those interrogations were so harsh that a number of the arrested people were ready to confess to what the NKVD wanted them to confess, even if they never did what they were accused of doing. They just wanted these harsh interrogations to stop, they could not take these interrogations anymore.

Maksim Isidorovich Gurevich told me that his father never confessed to things which he did not do. And later - he was released!

Professor M.I. Gurevich Treated Everybody With Equal Respect

Maksim Isidorovich told me that the example of how people should be treated with equal respect was given to him by S.A. Chaplygin.

S.A. Chaplygin (Sergei Alekseevich Chaplygin (1869-1942)) was Professor and Academician. When Maksim Gurevich, then a young mathematician, was hired by TsAGI, S.A. Chaplygin was, as far as I understand, the Head of the Theoretical Division of that Institution.

Chaplygin assigned Maksim Gurevich and one more young scientist to work out a solution to a certain problem of gliding over the surface of water. He gave the general directions on how to approach the problem, and these two young scientists had to work out all the details of the solution, to do all the necessary computations, etc.

It took Maksim Gurevich and his colleague one year to do that. Then they informed Chaplygin that the solution was ready. Chaplygin invited Maksim Gurevich to come to the place where he lived, on a certain day and at a certain time, to bring the solution and to show it to him.

When Maksim Gurevich came, there was another visitor in Chaplygin's apartment, a prominent scientist. (Maksim Isidorovich mentioned to me the name of that scientist, but I do not remember who that was.)

Chaplygin did not tell Maksim Gurevich to wait until he finished to discuss with that prominent scientist what they were discussing. To the contrary, he told that visiting scientist, "I allocated this time to our young colleague Maksim Gurevich. I am asking you to please go to my library room and to wait until Maksim Gurevich and I finish our conversation."

Two Good Russian Men

This story is about two good Russian men, each of whom, in different ways, helped a Jewish man to survive.

When my father served in the army as a field telephonist, one day he and another soldier were at their post, and their task was to maintain a telephone line in the working order. When the line was out of order, one of them - my father or another man - had to go, to find out why the line is not working, and to repair the line.

So it happened that the line stopped working again. It was the turn of my father to go and to bring the line to order. Another soldier, a Russian man, knew, however, that the boots of my father had holes in the soles, and it was raining, and he told my father, "Your boots are in the bad shape, you stay here, I shall go." And he went to repair the line.

He never came back. Telling us, my mother and me, this story, my father believed that this man possibly saved his life.

Another good Russian man: L.I. Sedov (Leonid Ivanovich Sedov (1907-1999)), Professor and Academician.

Above in this book, I described how Maksim Isidorovich Gurevich was suddenly expelled from TsAGI, and for two years, in the big city of Moscow, where there were tons of jobs for somebody with his qualifications, he could not get a job.

M.I. Gurevich and his wife, Irina L'vovna, had a small daughter, and the family needed money to live, of course. It was L.I. Sedov who helped M.I. Gurevich to survive those two years. In his authority, he was giving M.I. Gurevich various temporary works, like translations of scientific materials from English into Russian, for example, which was a source of income for M.I. Gurevich in those years.

I was not acquainted with L.I. Sedov. I saw him two times. One time he was making a presentation at the Institute for the Problems of Mechanics where I was then working. Another time, at the funeral of M.I. Gurevich.

L.I. Sedov showed himself a good Russian man.

Filia

When my mother lived in Odessa, one of her friends, a girl, had a brother whose name in his family was Filia. Once, when that girl and my mother came to the place where the family of that girl lived, my mother saw Filia walking along the room, back and forth, and talking. There was nobody in that room with whom Filia could talk, so my mother, surprised, ask that girl, "What is Filia doing?" "Oh," answered the girl, "Filia is studying mathematics."

The full name of Filia was F.R. Gantmaher (Feliks Ruvimovich Gantmakher (1908-1964)), and he became a well-known mathematician. My father mentioned to me the names of three mathematicians who taught him at the Odessa State University. One of them was M.G. Krein (Mark Grigor'evich Krein (1907-1989)), another one was F.R. Gantmakher, and the third name I do not remember.

By the way, when studying the mathematics subject of matrices, I used the monograph "Theory of Matrices," by F.R. Gantmakher.

Feliks Roziner

Feliks Roziner (1936-1997) was a writer. And he also was a friend of my childhood and teenage years and my classmate for all the years we were in school (1943-1953). He was one of three Jewish boys in my class in school.

Feliks' parents knew me well, and my parents knew Feliks well. Feliks' childhood name, and his name in his family, was Felik. My childhood name, and my name in my family, was Devik. I remember my parents holding Felik up as an example for me. "Look at Felik," they told me, "He is a good boy." Only many years later, when we were already adults, I learned - from Feliks - that his parents were holding me up as an example for him. "Look at Devik," they told him, "He is a good boy."

Feliks was a good pupil - in that sense that he usually got good or excellent grades. He was not what was called "otlichnik" (somebody who always, or almost always, gets A's), but he was a good pupil. For a period of time - in what grade of school that happened, I do not remember - he had problems with his heart. Maybe that was a complication after some ilness. So for that period of time, he was unable to come to class. He was in the bed, but somehow he continued to study, until his doctors allowed him to come to class again.

Feliks' parents and he lived in one room of an apartment, and they had neighbours living in the same apartment. (That was rather typical in the USSR.) That apartment was on the 8th (or on the 9th maybe) floor of some tall building, and it had a small balcony. Strangely, the only way to get to that balcony was through the window in the kitchen of the apartment. From that balcony, there was an unobstructed view in the direction of Red Square. I remember one time Feliks, and I, and somebody else also, tried to watch the military parade on Red Square on some November the 7th day, using a big binocular. The distance to Red Square was very large, and whether we could observe what was happening in the Square or not - I do not remember.

Above in this book, I wrote that before the school-leaving examination in mathematics, my father tutored me and two my classmates, who were my friends. One of those friends was Feliks Roziner. It was Feliks who, as I, received A for that examination, and it was Feliks who told me later that it was my father's choice of subjects and explanations that helped him to get A.

Feliks' parents had a book of a very large size in their apartment. The book was lying on a small table, it was simply impossibe to put that book on a shelf. Feliks mentioned that some ancestor (or ancestors maybe) owned, before the revolution of 1917, a store in Odessa named "Obrazovanie" ("Education"). That store was selling books (textbooks probably) and other things necessary in the process of educating or being educated.

(That store, by the way, is mentioned in the book "Beleet Parus Odinokii" ("A White Sail Gleams" or "Lonely White Sail") written by the well-known in the USSR writer Valentin Kataev (Valentin Petrovich Kataev (1897-1986)), who was born in Odessa and was a son of a teacher.)

As far as I remember, Feliks mentioned that that book was published by that ancestor (or by those ancestors). What was written in that book, I do not know. I never asked.

(Whether Feliks was able to take this book out of the USSR when he, at some point in his life, emigrated to Israel, I do not know. With few exceptions, to take a valuable thing out of the USSR, a person leaving the country permanently needed special permission. And he also had to pay the Soviet Government the sum of money equal to the value of that thing. Why was he required to pay that money - I never could understand. That thing was his property!

The Soviet Government also did not allow emigrants to take their money out of the USSR. With the exception of $120 per person. When my mother and I were leaving the USSR, 90 Soviet rubles were exchanged for $120 for each of us, and that was the only money we were allowed to take out of the country.)

When he was in school, Feliks read a lot. Well, eventually he became a writer. I also read a lot when I was in school. I did not become a writer, however. Probably, there was something different in his genes - that determined his interest to writing.

Whether Feliks tried to write poetry or prose when he was in school - I do not know. Maybe he did, but he never told me that. However, once Feliks gave me a present, a book, where four rhymed lines were written in his handwriting. That was either in the last grade of school or one or two years later. I do not have that book now, and I do not even remember what that book was about, but those four lines I remember. Here they are (in the transliteration):

V stepi razdavalsia topot i zvon,

Bezhalo stado bizonovo.

Vperedi bezhal s khvostom bizon,

Szadi - bizon bez onogo.

And here is my - a very imperfect - translation of these lines into English:

In the steppe, the clatter of hooves was heard,

That was the herd of bison running.

In front of the herd, there was a bison with tail,

A bison without tail - at the end of the herd.

All I can say about these four lines is that in the Russian language, they are rhymed very well. They are written in the style of the famous Soviet poet Vladimir Mayakovskii (Vladimir Vladimirovich Mayakovskii (1893-1930)). Was Feliks the author of these four lines or not? - I do not know. But I think that he was ...

After the high school, Feliks did not have a medal. So to become a student at an Institution of Higher Education, he needed to take the entrance examinations. He took the examinations and became a student at the Moscow Polygraphic Institute (today this institution is called the Moscow State University of Printing Arts), where he was educated as an engineer

(Incidentally, after the Mosrybvtuz was transferred to Kaliningrad, its building was turned over to the Moscow Polygraphic Institute. And for a short period of time, after I received my Kandidat Nauk Diploma, I was teaching Mathematics - at that Institute, in that building where I studied when I was a student. That was a second, part-time job for me. A woman who was selling refreshments in that building told me, "I remember you from the time when you were a student at Mosrybvtuz.")

Feliks was interested in Music and in the Art of Painting. I do not think that he tried to paint himself, but he definitely learned how to play two musical instruments: a stringed instrument called Domra (when he was in school) and, later in life, Violin.

Feliks married young, when he was a student at the Polygraphic Institute. He married a Jewish girl by the name Liudmila (Liuda); she was a student at the Polygraphic Institute too. Feliks and Liuda had one child, a son. (Who, I know, became a psychologist in Israel.)

Working as an engineer, Feliks nevertheless wanted to become a writer. He got a contract with some Publishing House in the Soviet Union to write a certain book (what book that was, I do not know). To write that book, Feliks quit his engineering job.

That could create a problem for him. To be a writer, not having any official job, in the USSR one had to be a Member of the USSR's Union of Writers (as far as I know).

Feliks was not a member of that Union. And the Soviet Government required all able men to have a job (or to be a student somewhere, or to have some other occupation recognized by the Government).

There was no unemployment in the Soviet Union, and if you needed a job, the authorities would find you one. Not necessarily what you would want to be your job, but a job nevertheless. If a man did not have an occupation recognized by the Government for a long period of time, he could have been arrested in the USSR.

And Feliks told me that the authorities (militsia maybe?) looked into the matter of why he was not working somewhere (after he quit his engineering job). Fortunately, the person who looked into that matter recognized the contract with a Publishing House that Feliks had, to write a book, as a valid reason for Feliks not to have an official job. That contract saved Feliks and allowed him to pursue his career as a writer.

When we were students at our respective Institutes, being educated (as engineers), Feliks and I were sometimes in contact. After we graduated and became engineers, we lost contact, and for a big number of years we knew nothing of each other's life.

One day, while in the Lenin Library, I came across Feliks. He was talking with a tall woman whom I did not know, and then she left, and I asked Feliks who that woman was. He answered that that woman was his wife.

I was very surprised. I knew his wife, Liuda. Feliks explained that he and Liuda divorced, and that that woman is his second wife, Tat'iana (Tania). Tania was a Russian woman, very well educated (she had a Ph.D.) and cultured.

We - Feliks and I - reestablished our connections, somewhat. I was in the apartment where he and Tania lived (in Moscow). On the wall, I saw a graph. I asked them, "What is that graph for?" They explained to me that that is the graph of the barometric pressure. It turned out that when the barometric pressure was too low, one of them had a headache. And when the barometric pressure was too high, another of them had a headache. So having that graph, they always knew whose turn it was to have a headache.

Feliks and Tania - together - did not have children. However, as far as I know from Tania, she had excellent relations with Feliks' first wife, Lyuda, and when Lyuda needed help with her and Feliks' son, Tania was always ready to help.

In May of 1977, the time came for me to go to the Central Office of OVIR, to receive my mother's and my visas for the exit from the Soviet Union, the Exit Visas. When I came to that office, to my great surprise, I saw, among people waiting to receive visas, Feliks and his father. It turned out that Feliks, and Tat'iana, and Feliks' father were going to emigrate to Israel.

After my mother and I emigrated to the United States, I lost contact with Feliks and Tat'iana and knew nothing of them for about ten years. In 1987 (most probably), when my mother and I lived in Fargo and I worked at NDSU, somebody gave us a few issues of the Russian-language newspaper Novoe Russkoe Slovo (The New Russian World) published in New York. Looking through the newspaper, my mother came across Feliks' name, Feliks Roziner.

I learned that Feliks is in the USA, found his address, sent him a letter, and received a response letter from him. Feliks and Tat'iana were living in Massachussets, near Boston. Tat'iana was a Faculty Member at Boston University, and Feliks continued writing his books and also worked as a Lecturer at Harvard. Feliks wrote to me in that letter that the years of life with Tat'iana were the best years of his life.

Feliks sent me a copy of one of his books, Lilovyi Dym (The Violet Smoke). I read that book. It was an interesting story, and well-written.

I learned that when living in Israel, Feliks developed a blood disease. Being treated in an Israeli hospital, he asked Tat'iana to bring him paper and writing instruments and continued writing the book which he was writing.

His doctors were able to suspend his disease at that time. However, years later the disease prevailed. In March of 1997, Feliks died. Tatyana called me over the telephone, and we talked, few times, in the period immediately after Feliks' death.

In the summer of 1997, Tat'iana sent me the book Feliks Roziner, "Izbrannoe" ("Selected Works"), published by the Terra Press, in Moscow, Russia, in 1996 (in the Russian language).

(By the way, I asked Tat'iana whether Feliks was the author of the four rhymed lines (which I cited above in this section). She did not know that. Still, I think he was.)

Eventually, we - Tat'iana and I - lost contact.

Feliks wrote his books in the Russian language. An English translation of his book "Nekto Finkel'maer" was published in the USA under the title "A Certain Finkelmeyer." Feliks' archives are now in the Amherst Center for Russian Culture, at Amherst College, in Amherst, Massachssets, USA.

I always remembered Feliks and Tat'iana, but my life was so, I would say, not-normal, so lacking good, positive events, that I thought I would contact Tat'iana later, when - and if - my life situation changed to the better.

When preparing this section of this book, with my memories of Feliks Roziner, I searched Google using his name. Then I learned that in 2009 Tat'iana died. After Feliks' death, she lived for twelve years.

In 2017, twenty years after Feliks' death, a book dedicated to his memory, entitled "Pamiati Feliksa Rozinera" ("To the Memory of Feliks Roziner"), was published in Swampscott, MA, by M-Graphics Publishing. It contains, in particular, memories of Feliks from a number of people who new him, including memories of his son and of his first wife, Liuda. The book is in the Russian languge.

I am not a specialist in literature, and my memories of Feliks Roziner are simple, as memories of a person who knew Feliks as a person.

Robert Robinson

When I lived in the Soviet Union, until some time after the Second World War I never saw a person with black skin. That is, I probably knew from books, or from school, that there were people whose skin was black, but I never met such a person until one day soon after the Second World War. Then I saw a man with black skin - for the first time.

That man worked at the ball-bearing factory, not far from where we then lived.

I never talked with that man, but my mother did talk with him. It turned out that he came to the USSR from the USA, sometime in the years of the Depression, for a job. The Soviet Government was offering jobs to foreign specialists, and he came. Then one day he became a citizen of the USSR. I do not know why he did that, but after he became the Soviet citizen, he was entrapped.

He had a mother, in America maybe (?), and he told my mother that he asked the Soviet authorities for the permission to go to visit his mother. "No," the authorities told him, "if you want to see your mother, invite her to come here to visit you." He was not married, and my mother asked him why he was not married. At that time, immediately after the Second World War, there was a big number of unmarried women in the USSR - because many more men were killed during the war than women.

He answered that he would marry an American woman, but not a Russian woman. And there were no American women around, of course. (I personally think that he maybe became disappointed in the life in the Soviet Union by that time, and maybe he wanted to get out of the USSR. And if he were married to a woman who was a Soviet citizen, it would be much more difficult for him to do that.)

That is practically all I knew about that man. I did not even know his name. Until recently.

One night, in June of 2016, I opened my eyes in the

middle of the night and turned on the radio. I was listening to a BBC broadcast, and they were talking about a black man who came to the USSR for a job during the Depression years, then became the Soviet citizen, and worked in Moscow at a ball-bearing factory.

I immediately realized that that was the same man whom I saw in Moscow soon after the Second World War, and with whom my mother talked. From that broadcast, I learned that his name was Robert Robinson, that in the 1970s, with the help of somebody from the Ugandian Embassy in Moscow, he moved to Uganda, Africa, and then moved to the United States, obtained the US Citizenship (which he lost when he accepted the Soviet Citizenship earlier), and that he died in 1994.

I also learned that he wrote a book about his life. On Amazon.com, I found information about that book. Its title is: "Black on Red: My 44 Years Inside the Soviet Union."

For all the years after the Second World War, I always remembered that man and remembered what he told my mother. I did not expect, however, that one day I will learn his name and anything new about him. But - improbable things happen sometimes in this life, and that I learned new things about him, seventy (or so) years after I saw him first in Moscow, is one of such improbable things, which happened.

Izrail' Hais

Izrail' Hais was a Jewish man and a friend of my father. As my father, he was born in the town of Rybnitsa in Moldavia. As my father's parents, his parents owned and operated a general store in the town of Rybnitsa, a smaller store. These two stores - my father's parents' store and

Izrail' Hais' parents' store - competed. The boys, however, my father and Izrail' Hais, became friends.

In his adult years, Izrail' Hais lived and worked in Kiev, the capital of the Ukrainian Republic in the USSR. One day, soon after the Second World War, he was in Moscow, and he found our address and came to visit us. (It was not difficult to find somebody's address in Moscow. There were special kiosks in Moscow where you could ask for the address of a person, and usually, after a short period of time, you were given that person's address.)

Izrail' Hais was an engineer. He worked at a factory in Kiev. What that factory was producing, I do not know. The only thing of that factory that I heard was that the director of the factory was a brother of L.M. Kaganovich (who was a close confederate of Stalin).

Izrail' Hais had no children of his own. I called him Uncle Izia, and my father and mother also started calling him Uncle Izia.

Uncle Izia came to Moscow from time to time, in connection with the business of the factory where he worked. Sometimes he stayed with us in our apartment during those, usually short, visits. He was a huge patriot of the country of Israel. His dream was to move to Israel. He told us, my parents and me, that he would better work as a blue-collar worker in Israel than as an engineer in the USSR.

He was not able to fulfill his dream. He died before my father died, sometime in 1976, or a little earlier.

Izrail' Hais was not a famous man. He was not a politician, not a writer, not an actor, not a famous scientist.

And his name is not on the Internet. But he was a man of a buoyant disposition and a huge patriot of the country of Israel.

He is one of the people who are not in this world anymore, but who are in my memory.

S. Shvartsburd

S. Shvartsburd was a relative of my father. By profession, he was a teacher of mathematics. Later in life, he became a Member of the Academy of Pedagogical Sciences of the USSR (I believe). What was his first name by his documents, I do not know. In our family, we called him - Suiasha.

When he was a child, something happened to his health, and he lost the ability to use his legs. For the rest of his life, he used crutches to move.

When he was a teenager, somebody (I think that was his mother) suggested that he should study watchmaking and become a watchmaker. That profession requires using one's eyes, hands, and brain, but it does not require using legs. He, however, had a different idea. He wanted to study mathematics and to become a mathematician. And that is what he did.

When I knew him, he was a teacher of mathematics, on the high school level, in one of the Moscow schools. In the building of that school, there was a basement apartment with the direct entrance to the school area. He lived in that apartment together with his mother, and later - together with his mother, his wife, and his daughter. Moving on crutches, he came to his classes to teach mathematics.

He was very active in the matter of the pedagogy of school mathematics. I believe that on that matter he was in contact with one of the very best mathematicians in the USSR, A.N. Kolmogorov (Andrei Nikolaevich Kolmogorov (1903-1987)), Professor and Academician, who also was interested in the pedagogy of school mathematics.

I just mentioned that Suiasha lived together with his mother. In our family, we called his mother - Aunt Leika.

(Aunt Leika was a relative of my father, but was she really his aunt or is that simply what we called her, I do not know. When we are young, we not always ask questions. And then, much later, the time comes when we would want to ask those questions, but there is nobody to ask.

My father had a sister, who died when she was seventeen, from tuberculosis. In our family, she was known simpy as "father's sister." Nobody ever mentioned her name. I have two photographs of her, and I would like to know what her name was. But there is nobody whom I can ask now.)

When the war between Germany and the USSR started, Aunt Leika lived in the area of the USSR adjacent to the country of Roumania. That area was occupied by the Roumanian Army. Roumanians created concentration camps for Jews (maybe Germans insisted on that?), and Aunt Leika was in one of those concentration camps. She told us that, unlike Germans, Roumanians were not killing Jews. And - she survived ...

It was in Suiasha's apartment that I first saw a television set and a television transmission. It was a black-and-white television with the screen of a very small size. In front of that screen, there was a lens (a glass lens or a plastic lense maybe) filled with the distilled water. Moving that lens, one could make the image on the screen of that tv to look bigger.

When we, my mother and I, left the Soviet Union, we lost contact with Suiasha, and I know nothing of his life after that.

Remark. *In addition to the Academy of Sciences of the USSR, there were also some specialized academies of sciences in the Soviet Union. The Academy of Pedagogical Sciences of the USSR was one of such specialized academies.*

Jewish Musicians from Odessa

When I mentioned (above in this book) the jazz-band leader Leonid Utesov, I stated that he was a Jew and originally from Odessa.

Not only he but some other leading musicians in the USSR at that time were Jews and originally from Odessa. Here are the ones of whom I knew: Emil' Gilel's, one of two best pianists in the USSR (another one was Sviatoslav Rikhter, not a Jew, and not originally from Odessa), David Oistrakh, the best violinist in the USSR, and Maria Grinberg, one of the leading pianists in the USSR.

I never met in person any of the musicians just named, with the exception of Maria Grinberg (Maria Izrailevna Grinberg (1908-1978)). From her Odessa time, my grandmother Hana knew the mother of Maria Grinberg, and my grandmother introduced me to that family. That was sometime in my high-school years.

Together with her mother and with her daughter (who was of about my age), Maria Grinberg lived in an apartment which was not sufficient for the needs of her family. One of the colleagues of Maria Grinberg wrote a letter to Stalin about that. After that, Maria Grinberg was given a different apartment, in one of the skyscapers which were built in Moscow in Stalin times. It was a much bigger apartment and better equiped than the apartments in which the ordinary Soviet citizens lived.

I just wrote that Maria Grinberg was *given* an apartment. One should know that at those times the apartments in the USSR belonged to the Goverment, and the Soviet citizens rented them from the Government. However, one could not simply come to a rental office and to rent an apartment. Usually, people were *given* apartments by the organizations where they worked, on a competitive basis.

There was a severe shortage of apartments in the USSR - because building apartment houses was not among the first priorities of the Soviet Goverment. A certain number of apartment houses were built, of course, but absolutely not sufficient for the needs of the population. The first priorities of the Soviet Goverment were the development of the heavy industry, building armaments, and everything connected to the cosmos (outer space) exploration.

In the later years, the Soviet citizens were allowed to buy apartments from the Government. Not many people had the means to buy an apartment, but some did.

My connection to the family of Maria Grinberg was short. When I entered Mosrybvtuz to study Naval Architecture, the study load was so heavy that I practically had no time for the social life in the first couple of years of studies. And I lost connection to that family. Looking back, I regret it.

Professor G.Yu. Stepanov

In the local (Fargo) Walmart store, there was a woman working, a cashier. Once that woman told me that when talking with me, she has a feeling that everything will be All Right. Similarly, when I talked with Professor G.Yu. Stepanov (Georgii Yur'evich Stepanov (1922-2005)), I always had strong positive feelings in my heart.

In the book Ref. [6], I already wrote about Professor Stepanov (see [6, pp. 107-108]). That book is a mathematics research book, written for the specialists. What is written about Georgii Yur'evich here is based mostly on what is written about him in that book.

I first met Professor G.Yu. Stepanov in 1964, when I was at Aspirantura of MIIT. He was Professor at the Military Armored Forces Academy in Moscow. He was associated with tanks all his adult life. When the Second World War started for the USSR, he was nineteen, and he was a member of a tank crew then. Later, he graduated from the Military Armored Forces Academy. He served in the Soviet Army, and his rank (when I knew him) was a colonel.

G. Yu. Stepanov was a man of quick mind, and he was a man of sharp mind too. M.I. Gurevich and G.Yu. Stepanov attracted my attention to the problem of the Jet Curtain of an Air-Cushion Vehicle, and since 1965, a number of my publications were connected to that problem.

Later, Professor G.Yu. Stepanov was one of the Opponents (Scientists whose task is to criticise and to evaluate) for my Dissertation. And it was on his and Professor Gurevich's recommendation that, after Aspirantura, I was offered a research job at the Institute for the Problems of Mechanics of the Academy of Sciences of the USSR (where I worked from 1966 to 1971).

I knew Georgii Yur'evich Stepanov from 1964 untill 1977. During those thirteen years, I saw him probably not more than ten or twelve times. A few times I talked with him on the telephone. And each time when I talked with him - in person or on the telephone - I had strong positive feelings in my heart. In 1977, I left the USSR and never communicated with him again.

They both, Maksim Isidorovich Gurevich and Georgii Yur'evich Stepanov, were noble men.

Herbert Grossman

When my mother and I emigrated to America, we did not know that we had relatives in the USA. We knew, however, that my mother had a cousin in South Africa. In our family, that cousin was called Abrasha. His first name was Abraham, and his last name was Grosman. By profession, he was an architect.

When Abrasha graduated, with a Diploma of an Architect, it was in the years of the Depression, and it was difficult for him to find a job. My grandmother Hana learned about that, and she wrote a letter to her brothers, who lived at that time in Ireland (or maybe in England). Her brothers found job for Abrasha in South Africa. That is how architect Abraham Grosman came to South Africa.

We - my mother and I - had the postal address of Abrasha in South Africa, but it was an old address. My mother wrote a letter to Abrasha and sent the letter (from Italy) to that old address. The South-African Postal Service found him, and my mother received a response letter.

Abrasha wrote that he remembered how my mother and he, being children, played in the sand. He gave us the address of a relative in England.

Abrasha's letter was written in the Russian language. He probably did not use, or almost did not use, that language during his life in South Africa. His Russian was far from perfect, but it was possible to understand everything in that letter.

Being in the USA, we contacted that relative from England, and he gave us the name and the address of our relative in the USA Herbert Grossman. Herbert Grossman lived on the East Coast of the USA. Sometime in 1978, we contacted him, and he invited us, my mother and me, to come and to spend a few days at the place where he lived.

I believe that our relationship with Herbert Grossman was as follows: one of his grandparents and my grandmother Hana Grossman were siblings in their family. I do not know how to describe this relationship in terms of what cousins we were, but somebody proficient in genealogy definitely can do that.

Herbert Grossman was a pharmacist, and he worked in executive positions for a number of pharmaceutical companies. He died in 1997, being at that time 67 years of age.

From his obituaries in the New York Times and in the Washington Post, I learned that he participated in the introduction of some important medicines, such as the polio vaccine and valium.

Herbert and his wife Sandra had three daughters. Ms. Robin Mangino, mentioned in pages 6 and 7 of this book, is their oldest daughter.

I deeply regret that Herbert is not alive. From all the people whom I met in the United States, I felt closest to him.

Chapter 6

Other Stories

Meanings of the Word Class (in School)

In the USA, if a group of pupils graduated from a certain school in the year 2003, for example, that group is called Class of 2003 of that school. The word Class (in School) can also mean a group of pupils learning the same subjects together (in the USA).

In the USSR, the word Class (in School) meant only the group of pupils learning the same subjects together. (There was no such a notion as Class of a certain year of a school - in the USSR.)

Meaning of the Word Nationality

The meaning of the word Nationality in the Soviet Union was also different from the meaning of that word in the USA.

In the USA, if you are born in this country, your nationality is: American. In the Soviet Union, there was no such nationality as Soviet. The nationality of a person was his ethnicity.

In the USSR, citizens had to have passports. In the USA, a passport is necessary if you are going abroad. In the USSR, a passport was necessary for life in the country.

In the USSR, a person was issued passport at the age of

sixteen. In that document, there were different items. The item number five was - your nationality. The most numerous nationality in the Soviet Union was: Russian. Other nationalities were: Ukrainian, Belorussian, Kazakh, Tajik, Georgian, German, Jew, and many other nationalities.

The nationality of a person was determined by the nationalities of his parents. If both parents - of a son or a daughter - were of the same nationality, that determined the nationality of their son or daughter. If the parents had different nationalities, a young person, son or daughter, could choose nationality of one of the parents to be his or her nationality.

On the Discrimination Against Jews in the USSR

In the Russian Empire, the predecessor of the USSR, the restrictions on Jews and the discrimination against Jews were of the religious nature. If a person of the Jewish Religion was willing to change his religion and to become Christian, and did it - after that, the restrictions and the discrimination against that person no longer existed!

The cases when Jews in the Russian Empire were willing to change their religion and to become Christians were, I believe, extremely rare. I heard of one such case when a Jew who was a talented Opera Singer was offered the job of a singer at an Opera House in a big city, in Moscow or in Saint Petersburg maybe, where Jews were not allowed to live. In order to be able to fulfill his dream and to work in Opera, he changed his religion and became Christian. Did it really happen, and who that singer was - I do not know. But that is what I heard.

In the Soviet Union, my father told me, there was no

discrimination against Jews before the Second World War. In the sense that people of the Jewish nationality had the same opportunity to be admitted to the Institutions of Higher Education or to be given jobs - as people of other nationalities. The discrimination against Jews in the USSR started after the Second World War.

Father told me that during the war German airplanes sometimes dropped leaflets. One of these leaflets showed a number of Jewish people who were in the positions of authority in the USSR, and it was written, "Russian people, look who rules you! Jews rule you!" (Or something like that was written in that leaflet.)

I do not know how many Jews were in the positions of power in the USSR during the time of the Second World War. My memory pertains to the time after that war, and searching in my memory, I see only two names of Jews on the top of the Soviet political or industrial leadership: L.M. Kaganovich and V.E. Dymshits.

The ruler (the dictator) in the Soviet Union was Stalin (Iosif Vissarionovich Stalin, Joseph Stalin). Next to him, there was a group of people, not big in number group of people, and L.M. Kaganovich (Lazar' Moiseevich Kaganovich) was one of these people, and he was very close to Stalin. V.E. Dymshits (Veniamin Emmanuilovich Dymshits) was one level lower (I would say) but also on a high level of leadership. There is information about these two individuals, Kaganovich and Dymshits, on the Internet, so I will not go into details about them here.

My father also told me that the soldiers of his artillery unit were asking him, "Lieutenant, why don't we see Jews in the army?" "How," my father was answering, "I am a Jew, and I am with you!" "Well," soldiers told him, "you, of course, but where are other Jews?" They probably did not understand that Jews were a small minority of the population, and their number in the army could not be big, but in proportion with their number in the total population of the Soviet Union. Jews could not be seen as often as the people of the more numerous nationalities.

The German propaganda during the Second World War probably played a certain role in increasing anti-semitism in the Soviet Union.

The discrimination against Jews in the USSR (which started after the Second World War) increased - after the creation of the country of Israel. The USSR was the first country to recognize Israel de jure. However, after Israel became an internationally recognized country, a number of Jews from the Soviet Union wanted to emigrate to Israel. Stalin probably did not like that. In his mind, I think, the USSR was the best country in the world. So the idea that anybody from the Soviet Union would want to leave the country and to emigrate to Israel was not an acceptable idea for Stalin.

The discrimination against Jews in the USSR - in admittance to the Institutions of Higher Education or in obtaining jobs - was based strictly on what was the nationality of a person as it was written in his or her passport. If according to your passport your nationality was a Jew, you were discriminated against, period.

Here are two examples of how the Jewish identity of a person was concealed (in the Soviet Union) - in order for that person to be treated without discrimination or prejudice.

In the section Some Vacations, above, I mentioned a

daughther of my relatives in Rybnitsa who was of my age. When she graduated from the high school in Rybnitsa, she wanted to study physics and to became a physics teacher. To study physics, she applied for admittance to some University. She was a Jewess. That could influence negatively her chance to be admitted.

Her first name and patronymic (about patronymics, please see Appendix One) were Maria Peretsovna. Her first name, Maria, did not suggest that she was a Jewess. And her last name (which I am not citing here) also did not suggest that she was a Jewess. But her patronymic, Peretsovna, meant that the first name of her father was Perets, and that suggested that her father was a Jew.

Maria's parents did not want the Admitting Committee (at that University) to know that Maria was a Jewess. So they persuaded a secretary at the University to type Maria's first name and patronymic, on the list of the applicants, as Maria Petrovna. Petrovna meant that the first name of her father was Petr (Peter), and that was a common Russian name (think of Peter the Great, for example). Maria was admitted, graduated from that University, and became a physics teacher.

A somewhat similar situation occured in the life of one of my Mosrybvtuz classmates. He had to defend his Kandidat Nauk (Ph.D.) Dissertation at some Research Institute in Moscow. He was a Jew, and his first name and patronymic were Il'ia Ruvimovich. His first name, Il'ia, did not suggest that he was a Jew. His last name (which I am not citing here) also did not suggest that. However, his patronymic, Ruvimovich, meant that the first name of his father was Ruvim, and that meant that his father was a Jew.

The person who was in charge of the defense of Il'ia's

dissertation at that Research Institute was a good man, and he probably thought that the fact that Il'ia was a Jew could influence his defense negatively. So when reading aloud Il'ia's first name and patronymic, he pronounced them as Il'ia Romanovich. Romanovich meant that the first name of Il'ia's father was Roman, and that was a Russian-sounding name.

Unusual things were done sometimes in the environment of the Soviet Union.

Jewish Life in Moscow?

An acquaintance of mine, a Jew born and raised in the United States, asked me to describe to him the Jewish life in Moscow, USSR.

The Jewish life in Moscow? When I was growing up, in the 1940s and 1950s, and later (my mother and I left the Soviet Union in 1977), there was practically no Jewish life in Moscow! There were no Jewish schools where young Jewish boys and girls could learn the Jewish languages, Yiddish or Ivrit (Hebrew), or the Jewish culture. There was no Jewish Club where Jews could socialize. (As far as I know, there were no other ethnic clubs in Moscow either.) The Jews of Moscow were, I would say, disunited.

The Jewish culture was suppressed. In the very first years after the Second World War, one could buy a newspaper in the Yiddish language in the newspaper kiosks in Moscow. My father, who knew both the Yiddish and the Ivrit languages, sometimes bought and read that newspaper. Later, the newspaper disappeared. Until sometime in 1948, there was a Jewish Theater in Moscow, where plays were performed in Yiddish. Then the authorities closed that theater.

This is how my father learned about that. He and my mother, who also could speak Yiddish, were sometimes buying tickets to the Jewish Theater and enjoying plays in Yiddish. One day in 1948, my father came to the theater tickets kiosk in the vestibule of one of the Moscow Metro stations and told the clerk that he wanted to buy two tickets to the Jewish Theater. "There is no such theater in Moscow," answered the clerk. The Jewish Theater was closed, and its building was given to some theater performing in the Russian language.

On extremely rare occasions, one could listen to a Jewish song on the radio. The singer, M.D. Aleksandrovich (Mikhail Davidovich Aleksandrovich (1914-2002)), was a Jew, and he had a wonderful voice.

The Jewish population of Moscow was about two hundred thousand, or two hundred fifty thousand in number. And there was only one Synagogue in the city. It was located on some lane in the center (downtown) of Moscow. On the day of Yom Kippur (the day of Atonement), that lane, in front of the Synagogue building, was packed with Jews. Religious, and not religious - they were coming to emphasize their Jewish identity, to demonstrate that they are Jews!

Knockers

In the Soviet Union, the KGB (the secret police) had, I believe, informants in all the layers of the Soviet Society. These people were the eyes and the ears of that organization. There was a special name for these people in the unofficial Russian language of the Soviet times, "stukachi." The best I can translate this word, "stukachi," into the English language is "knockers." Why they were called knockers, I do not know, but your friend could be such a knocker - and you would never know that, because he would never tell you that.

I think that some such knockers entered the United States with the wave of the Jewish Immigration. And I think they probably continued their collaboration with the KGB. I have no proof of that, of course. But that is what I think, that is my opinion.

Higher Education in the USSR

In the USSR, the system of higher education was different from the system of higher education in the USA.

In the USA, there is the four-year higher education after the high school, and there is the four-year degree called the Bachelor's Degree. In the USSR, there was no four-year higher education after the high school, and there was no degree corresponding to the Bachelor's Degree in the USA.

Most of the institutions providing higher education in the USSR were called Institutes. Some were called Universities.

At Universities, students studied the fundamental sciences: physics, mathematics, chemistry, biology, etc. Also - law, linguistics, and some other disciplines. Universities did not teach, however, engineering, music, medicine, etc. These subjects were taught at Institutes, and the Institutes were specialized. An Institute of the Oil and Gas Industry would teach all the subjects connected to oil and gas, but not the subjects pertinent to rare metals, for instance. To teach the subjects pertinent to rare metals, different Institute(s) existed.

The duration of the education of an engineer (after high

school) in the USSR was typically five years, in the case of the more difficult to learn engineering professions - five-and-a-half years. The duration of the University education in the USSR was six years (after high school).

People who graduated from Institutes (five, or five-and-a-half year degrees), or from Universities (six year degrees) could then continue their education at Aspirantura, an equivalent to the Ph.D. program in the USA. With the restriction that people with the Engineering Diplomas were not allowed to enter Aspirantura immediately after receiving their Diplomas. They were required to have at least two years of experience of work in industry, as engineers, before entering Aspirantura.

The duration of the Aspirantura education was three years, and a person who graduated from Aspirantura and defended Dissertation was called Kandidat Nauk (Candidate of Sciences).

Kandidat Nauk is a Doctoral degree equivalent to the Ph.D. degree in the USA. Obtaining Kandidat Nauk degree was based mostly on research.

Now, in the USA there exists only one Doctoral degree, called Ph.D. In the USSR, there were two Doctoral degrees. The second one, higher than the Kandidat Nauk degree, was called Doktor Nauk (Doctor of Sciences) degree. The program leading to that degree was called Doktorantura. Obtaining that degree was also based mostly on research.

In the USA, an equivalent to the Doktor Nauk degree does not exist, and an equivalent to Doktorantura does not exist too.

Education in the USSR was fundamental. For example, when studying mathematics, students were required to deliver the proofs of all the necessary theorems and lemmas - in addition to being able to solve problems.

(That fundamental education influenced the style of my teaching. A student of the North Dakota State University wrote in his evaluation, "Dr. Tselnik makes things fundamental, and when they are fundamental, they are easier to understand and easier to learn." I cite this - from memory.)

When Jews from the USSR started to emigrate to Israel, Israel had to study the Soviet System of Higher Education. In Israel, the system of the higher education degrees is the same as in the USA: Bachelor's degree, Master's degree, and Ph.D. degree. The Israeli authorities needed to know to which Israeli degrees the diplomas and the degrees from the Soviet Union were equivalent.

They came to the conclusion that in particular the Diplomas of Engineers from the Soviet Union are equivalent to the Master's degrees, in the corresponding fields of engineering, from the Israeli Institutions of Higher Education.

In Conclusion

In one of the sections of this book, I cited a small verse which I wrote when I was about fourteen years of age. In that verse, I write that usually - not always but usually - life is very sad. And that life can be compared to a branch of a lone tree, which the wind flutters and shakes.

Well, was my life sad? No, no, and no again!

That is because from the age of about sixteen-and-a-half, I was deeply engrossed in studies and then in research. I had no time for sadness in my life.

When I submitted the manuscript of the first edition of this book to the printer, I was seventy-six, close to seventy-seven. Today, I am eighty-one. Until about seventy-nine, I felt myself relatively healthy. Until that time, I had no serious health problems.

However, as they say in the Russian language,

Starost' ne radost',
A molodost' gadost'.

Or, in my approximate translation into English,

Old age is not a joy age,
But young age is just a junk age.

With respect to the young age, this is a joke, of course. With respect to the old - partially that is true. Because when we are old, various diseases attack us.

As I just wrote, until about seventy-nine, I felt myself relatively healthy. Since seventy-nine, that changed for me. In particular, in 2017 I had three, as I call them, health disasters, and I spent six months in a hospital and in two nursing homes.

After that, I came home, where I now live, and where I can do things, write this book, for example. With the help of my friends, I am recovering.

Was my life lonely? Partially, yes.

I was married, from the age of about twenty, for about eight-and-a-half years. Then I divorced and never married again. (That was kind of strange. Indeed, when I was born, a nurse told my mother, "Your son has double crown on his head. He will have two wives." Well, that nurse was only half-right. Was she a well-qualified nurse?)

I was divorced, but while both my parents lived, and later, while my mother lived, I did not feel lonely. After my mother died, in 1987, more years than not - I was lonely.

I do have a daughter. I already wrote about her in this book. She is fifty-nine years old now. Of these fifty-nine years, we were in contact for about twenty-two years only. In particular, before 2018, my daughter did not call me for about sixteen years. Before these sixteen years, she did not call me for about three years. My daughter has a daughter too, my granddaughter.

My friends from Fargo found my granddaughter, in Israel. In January of 2018, she called me, and I talked with her and with my daughter. I heard my daughter weeping on the phone. She felt guilty, and she told me that. "I am glad that you said that," I answered.

What happened in the past, people cannot change. Today we - my daughter, my granddaughter, and I - communicate. I also talked with my son-in-law, the husband of my daughter.

God's ways are inscrutable. And that is true - independently of whether you believe in the existence of God or not.

D.S. Tselnik.

Appendix One

About the Names of My Parents, About My Name, and the Dates of Our Lives

First of all, I have to explain that the way of naming people was different in the Russian Empire and in the USSR from what is customary in the United States.

In the United States, when a baby is born, the baby is usually given two names: the first name and the middle name.

In the Russian Empire and in the USSR, babies usually were given only one name, their first name. Instead of the middle name, people had what was called "otchestvo" - the patronymic. The patronymic of a person is the first name of that person's father, but slightly changed. For example, if the first name of the father is Izrail', then the patronymic is Izrailevich (for a man) or Izrailevna (for a woman).

The Jewish first name of my father was Isroel. In his (Soviet) documents, the name of my father was written as Srul' Shlemovich Tsel'nik. In everyday life, my father was addressed as Izrail' Solomonovich.

The Jewish first name of my mother was, I believe, Malka. In her documents in the USSR, my mother's name was written as Maria Ovseevna Spivak.

My Jewish name is David ben Isroel (David, son of Isroel). In the documents in the USSR, my name was written as David Srulevich Tsel'nik. In everyday life, I was addressed as David Izrailevich. (My childhood name, and my name in my family, was Devik.)

When my mother and I were leaving the Soviet Union, our names were translated into English in the Austrian Embassy (or in the Austrian Consulate maybe) in Moscow. My mother's name was translated as Marya Spivak, and my name was translated as David Tselnik. These translations became our legal names in the USA.

The research articles which I published when I lived in the USSR were published under the name D.S. Tsel'nik. In the USA, I used the names D.S. Tselnik, or David S. Tselnik - when publishing my research articles or books written by me.

And now, the dates of our lives.

My father was born on 1 December 1910. He died, in Moscow, USSR, on 25 November 1976.

My mother was born on 23 December 1909. She died, in Fargo, North Dakota, USA, on 16 December 1987.

I was born on 17 January 1937.

By the way, my first name, David, was suggested by my mother. She was reading the book "David Copperfield," by Charles Dickens, and she liked that name.

Incidentally, during all my life in the USSR, I never met another man or boy named David! I came across a number of Davids in the USA, however.

Appendix Two

Editions in Which the Research Articles Written by Me (by the Author of This Book) Were Published

Twenty-seven research articles written by me were published. Twenty of them were published in journals.

Here is the list of these journals:

1. *Proceedings (Izvestia) of the Academy of Sciences of the USSR, Mechanics.*
2. *Fluid Dynamics.*
3. *Journal of Applied Mathematics and Mechanics (PMM).*
4. *Journal of Hydronautics.*
5. *Journal of Ship Research.*
6. *Elemente der Mathematik.*
7. *Complex Variables Theory and Application.*
8. *Applied Mathematics Letters.*
9. *Computers and Mathematics with Applications.*
10. *Journal of Mathematical Analysis and Applications.*
11. *SIAM Journal on Mathematical Analysis.*

The first journal on this list is in the Russian language. One article was published in that journal. That article is available in the Russian language only.

Nineteen published in journals research articles are

available in the English language.

Other seven research articles were published in the following editions:

12. *Transactions of the Moscow Institute of Railway Engineering* (MIIT, Moscow, USSR).
13. *Transactions of the 8th USSR Conference in Shells and Plates Theory* (Rostov-on-Don, USSR).
14. *Transactions of the All-Union Research and Development Institute for Total Automation of the Oil and Gas Industry* (Moscow, USSR).
15. *Problems of Applied Mathematics and Mechanics* (Chuvash State University, Cheboksary, USSR).

The articles published in these editions are available in the Russian language only.

The List of my twenty-seven published research articles is given in Ref. [5, pp. 383-385].

Appendix Three

Some Positive Opinions of Me

* This is from a student (of NDSU) evaluation of me, "Dr. Tselnik can smile and mean it."

* This is from the letter of recommendation (for me) written by a former Chair of the Mathematics Department of NDSU, "David is a quiet individual with a wry sense of humour that students appreciate."

* In 1991, my daughter, who then lived in Moscow, the USSR, came on my invitation to Fargo, ND and spent three months with me. After many years that we did not communicate, she practically did not know me as a human being. After spending some time with me, she told, "Father, you are very sincere."

   (She also told that she understood how much she lost because when growing up, she did not have me in her life.)

* Some time ago, at a Walmart store in Fargo, I wanted to buy a box of Cacao Powder. There were boxes of cacao of two different brands, and I wanted to understand the difference between these two products. A young woman was standing nearby, and I asked her a question about that. It turned out that she was a nutritionist, working at the Sanford Medical Center in Fargo. We talked, and then I put one of the boxes in my cart, and the woman left.

   Some time later, I was in the Sanford Medical Center on Broadway in Fargo and was walking, and a woman, who was walking in the opposite direction, approached me. She reminded me that we had met at Walmart and talked. "I was touched," she told, mentioning that our conversation.

Now it was my turn to be touched ...

*   Recently, I came to the Sanford Clinic on Broadway in Fargo. The receptionist at the Internal Medicine Department, a young woman, greeted me by my first name. I did not remember that receptionist, and I was surprised that she knew my name. "How do you know my name?" I asked. "You leave a deep impression on people," she answered, "and that is why I remember your name."

I was astonished. Very pleasantly astonished, I have to say.

Glossary

Academician - Full Member of the Academy of Sciences of the USSR.

Aspirantura - Program of studies and research leading to the degree of Kandidat Nauk.

Aspirant - Person who studies and does research at Aspirantura.

Assistent - Assistant Professor.

Bauman Moscow Higher Technical School - Baumanskii Institute; today - Bauman Moscow State Technical University.

Bol'shoi - Big, Large.

Bukhgalter - Accountant or Book-keeper.

Center of City - Downtown.

Delo Vrachei - Doctor's plot.

Diploma Project - Project which a student of an Institution of Higher Education (in the USSR) had to do and to defend - to receive his Diploma.

Director of School - Principal of School.

Dotsent - Associate Professor.

Fakul'tet - College.

Gosstrakh - State Insurance (National Insurance).

Kamenets-Podolsk - City in the USSR where the author of this book was born. Today - city in Ukraine. Also called Kamenets-Podol'sk, Kamenets-Podolski, or Kamianets-Podilskyi.

Kandidat Nauk - USSR's equivalent to Ph.D. degree in the Western World.

Keta - Variety of the fish salmon.

Kvass - Russian non-alcoholic beverage.

Long-Long Hair - translated into the English language, an expression of the Russian language meaning: very long hair.

Mekhanico-Mathematical Fakul'tet of the Moscow State University - College of Mechanics and Mathematics of the Moscow State University.

Metro - The Underground (called Subway in the USA, Tube in London).

MIIT - Moscow Institute of Engineers of Railway Transport; today - Moscow State University of Railway Engineering.

Militsia - Police.

Militsioner - Policeman.

Mosrybvtuz - Moscow Technical Institute of the Fish Industry and Economy.

NDSU - North Dakota State University (in Fargo, ND, USA).

NKVD - People's Commissariat for Internal Affairs. (Included a predecessor of the KGB.)

Odessa - City in the USSR, on the shore of the Black Sea. Today - city in Ukraine.

OVIR - Department of Visas and Registration.

Pale of Settlement - A region of the Russian Empire where Jewish people were allowed to live.

Practice - Summer-time learning practice of a student at a factory, at a design bureau, at a research institution, etc.; Internship.

Pro-Rector - Vice Rector, Vice Head.

PT&E Committee - Promotion, Tenure, and Evaluation Committee.

Pupils - In the USSR, those who studied in schools (grades 1-10 in the USSR) were not called "students" but were called by the Russian equivalents of the word "pupils."

R&D - Research and Development.

Rector of a University (an Institute) - Head of a University (an Institute).

Rukovoditel' - Leader.

School-Leaving Examinations - Examinations for obtaining the High-School Diploma.

State University - in the USA, University of a certain State; in the USSR, National University.

Students - In the USSR, "students" were called those who studied at the Institutions of Higher Education, after the high school but below the level of Aspirantura.

Torgsin - Trade With Foreigners.

TsAGI - Central Aerohydrodynamics Institute.

UILO - Ukrainian Institute for the Linguistic Education (in Kiev, the Ukrainian Republic, USSR).

VCSU - Valley City State University (in Valley City, ND, USA).

Voenkomat - Military Commissariat.

Vostok - East.

References

1. G. Birkhoff and E.H. Zarantonello, "Jets, Wakes, and Cavities," Academic Press, New York, 1957.
2. M.I. Gurevich, "Theory of Jets in Ideal Fluids," The State Publishing House of the Physico-Mathematical Literature, Moscow, 1961 (in Russian).
3. M.I. Gurevich, "Theory of Jets in Ideal Fluids," Academic Press, New York, 1965.
4. M.I. Gurevich, "The Theory of Jets in an Ideal Fluid," Pergamon Press (International Series of Monographs in Pure and Applied Mathematics, Vol. 93), Oxford, UK, 1966.
5. D.S. Tselnik, "Six Chapters on Series Expansions," Published By The Author, Fargo, North Dakota, USA, 2012.
6. D.S. Tselnik, "The Function Xi_{*}," Published by David Tselnik, Fargo, North Dakota, USA, 2013.

Table of Contents

Preface to the Third Edition	Page 5
From the Preface to the Second Edition	7
From the Preface to the First Edition	7

Part One.   INJUSTICE.

Chapter 1. In The USSR.

My Parents and Grandparents	10
1937 - I Am Born; 1939 - Our Family Moves to Moscow	11
Before the Second World War Started for the USSR	13
Germany Invades the Soviet Union. My Father Is Drafted into the Soviet Army; Mother and I Are Evacuated from Moscow	14
Mother and I Return to Moscow; I Enter the First Grade of School	17
At a Young Age, I Learned That I Could Be Disliked Just for Being a Jew	18
End of the War	19
My Father Returns Home from the Army	21
1953 - I Finish High School	22
1953 Was the Most Difficult Year for a Jew To Be	

Admitted to an Institution of Higher Education	24
I Am Admitted To Study Naval Architecture (Shipbuilding)	29
I Want To Learn More Mathematics	31
My Father's Advice Was Invaluable to Me	32
I Graduated, I Am a Naval Architect. But Being a Jew, the Prestigious Research Institute TsAGI Did Not Hire Me	33
I Am Required To Study Welding Engineering	33
I Work as an Engineer; I Continue My Self-Studies of Mathematics	36
After the Years of Self-Studies of Mathematics, My Main Goal Is To Do Research	37
I Am Admitted to Aspirantura (Ph.D. Program)	39
Years at Aspirantura	42
I Am Kandidat of Physico-Mathematical Sciences (Ph.D., in Physico-Mathematical Sciences)	45
About My Research During the Years of Aspirantura	46
After Aspirantura	47
TsAGI Does Not Hire Me Again. This Time, I Knew Exactly Why: the KGB Did Not Allow To Hire Me	48
After the Institute for the Problems of Mechanics	49
I Want To Leave the Soviet Union	50

Chapter 2. In The USA.

My Mother and I Leave the Soviet Union	51
We Are in the USA	52
Temporary Jobs and the Beginning of My Research Activity in the USA	52
We Are the Naturalized Citizens of the USA, but I Am Not Given Security Clearance	54
About My Daughter	55
Permanent Job for Me Is Found - at the North Dakota State University (NDSU), in Fargo, North Dakota	56
Working at NDSU	57
My Mother Dies	58
Tenure Consideration - for Me, at NDSU - Begins. The PT&E Committee Recommends Not To Grant Me Tenure	59
Good News: My Second Submitted from NDSU Research Article Is Highly Recommended for Publication	61
Reconsideration of My Tenure Starts, but Quickly Stalls	62
My Second Submitted from NDSU Research Article Is Accepted for Publication. I Am Denied Tenure at NDSU	63
Some Things in Life Can Be Understood but Not	

Proved	64
Three of My Research Articles - Submitted After My Job at NDSU Ended - Are Published. I Talk With Dean Allan Fischer	65
I Try To Return to NDSU; Four More of My Research Articles Are Published	66
After 1997 - Not One of My Research Articles Was Published	67
I Discover New Things About My Tenure Consideration - Several Years After the Events	68
Documents About My Teaching at NDSU	70
Acting Dean Dr. Allan Ashworth, Describing My Teaching at NDSU, Distorted the Truth	73
Additional Documents About My Teaching at NDSU Were Included With My Tenure Dossier	75
Interim Vice-President for Academic Affairs of NDSU Dr. Allan Fischer Could (and Should) Interfere, but He Did Nothing	78
I Discover New Things About My Tenure Consideration - Several Years After the Events (Continued)	78
On the Matter of Tenure	79
Looking Back	81
A Guy Tells That I Have Problems With People From Lebanon	81
One-Semester Job: Teaching Mathematics at the Valley City State University	83

One-Semester Part-Time Job: Teaching Statics at the Department of Mechanical Engineering of NDSU	85
No, I Am Not a Mechanical Engineer	86
No, I Am Not an Architect	87
About Hearing Loss, Macular Degeneration, and Diabetes	88
My Research Interests - During the Years of Work at NDSU and in the Later Years	89
What Is Applied Mathematics?	90
I Wrote and Published a Mathematics Research Book	93
As a Mathematician, I Am an Applied Mathematician	94
My Second Mathematics Research Book	94
Again, Looking Back	94
As a Scientist	95

Part Two. OTHER RECOLLECTIONS.

Chapter 3. More About The Events In My Life.

When I Was Two-and-a-Half, and When I Was Five	98
Story of the Stolen Flounder	99
Story of the Piano Which I Never Got	100

Some Memories of the Time of the Second World War	101
Shoes	103
Satchel	103
Another Case of Anti-Semitism	103
Ice Cream	104
Commercial Food Stores	105
Buying Bread Without Coupons	105
Abundance of Food	106
Greek Olives	107
Going to the Bathhouse	108
Short-Wave Radio-Receivers	110
When I Was Eleven	113
When I Was Thirteen	113
When I Was Fourteen	114
Fountain-Pens	114
Foreign-Made Cars	117
Pastry Shop Einem	119
Eliseevskii Store	121
Studying the English Language	122
Helping My Mother in Her Work	124
French Buns, City Buns, and Related Matters	125
Tarzan Movies and Other American Movies Which I Saw in the USSR	126
She and I, Combinedly, Saw Two Tyrants: Stalin and Hitler	127
Ballroom Dancing	129

Photography	132
Some Vacations	133
When Stalin Died	137
Sport, Books, and the Moscow Libraries	138
Engineering Drawing	140
Studying Higher Mathematics at Mosrybvtuz	141
Sailing Practice	144
Other Practices and the Diploma Project	147
On the Colors: Green and Red	151
On Teaching	152
On Grades, Grading, and on the Teaching Load in Schools	155
Studying Mathematics on My Own	156
In Reserve of the Soviet Navy	157
Gout	159
Concert of a Japanese Jazz-Band	160
Counting Committee	161
Scientific Presentations and Falling in Love	162
Socks of Different Colors on My Right and Left Feet, Etc.	163
Long Vacation	165
Engineering Computations	167
How I Gambled and Lost Money in Las Vegas	170
My Bowling Experience	171
Crossing USA by Bus	172
About Some Cities Where I Was	173
On the Matter of Food	177

Chapter 4. Some Events In The Lives Of My Grandparents And Parents.

More About My Grandparents	179
Story of a Destroyed Dream	185
My Mother Originally Wanted To Become a Medical Doctor	186
For a Period of Time, My Mother Wanted To Become a Translator	188
Lack of Food	189
Voenkomat and the Pregnancy of My Mother	190
Spy in the Hat!	190
Two War Front Experiences of My Father	191

Chapter 5. Stories About Other People.

Professor M.I. Gurevich, a Jew, Was Born in Moscow, Russia, in 1909	193
Professor V.V. Stepanov's Advice	193
Professor M.I. Gurevich Treated Everybody With Equal Respect	195
Two Good Russian Men	196
Filia	197
Feliks Roziner	198
Robert Robinson	206
Izrail' Hais	208

S. Shvartsburd	210
Jewish Musicians from Odessa	212
Professor G.Yu. Stepanov	214
Herbert Grossman	215

Chapter 6. Other Stories.

Meaning of the Word Class (in School)	218
Meaning of the Word Nationality	218
On the Discrimination Against Jews in the USSR	219
Jewish Life in Moscow?	223
Knockers	224
Higher Education in the USSR	225

In Conclusion 228

Appendix One

About the Names of My Parents, About My Name, and the Dates of Our Lives	231

Appendix Two

Editions in Which the Research Articles Written by Me (by the Author of This Book)

Were Published	233

Appendix Three

Some Positive Opinions of Me	235
Glossary	237
References	240

Books Published by David Tselnik

D.S. Tselnik, "Six Chapters on Series Expansions," Published By The Author, Fargo, North Dakota, USA, 2012. (401 pp., Hardcover.)

D.S. Tselnik, "The Function Xi_*," Published by David Tselnik, Fargo, North Dakota, USA, 2013. (114 pp., Softcover.)

D.S. Tselnik, "Life of a Scientist: My Life in the USSR and in the USA," Published by David Tselnik, Fargo, North Dakota, USA, 2014. (97 pp., Softcover.)

D.S. Tselnik, "Life of a Scientist: My Life in the USSR and the USA," Second Edition, Expanded, Published by David Tselnik, Fargo, North Dakota, USA, 2018. (172 pp., Softcover.)

D.S. Tselnik, "Life of a Scientist: My Life in the USSR and the USA. Injustice and Other Recollections," Third Edition, Further Expanded, Published by David Tselnik, Fargo, North Dakota, USA, 2019. (252 pp., Softcover.)